Cornish Feasts and Festivals

Liz Woods
illustrations Freya Laughton

Alison Hodge

For my mother and hers, and so on…

First published in 2013 by
Alison Hodge, 2 Clarence Place, Penzance,
Cornwall TR18 2QA, UK
info@alison-hodge.co.uk
www.alisonhodgepublishers.co.uk

Reprinted 2014

ISBN-13 978-0-906720-87-5

British Library Cataloguing-in-Publication Data
A catalogue record for this book is available from
the British Library.

Edited by Yvonne Bristow

Designed and originated by
BDP – Book Development and Production,
Penzance, Cornwall

Printed in China

Title page: Tea treat saffron buns.

Contents

Introduction

In January 2010 I delivered a late Christmas present to my friend Jenni, who lives near Zennor in the far west of Cornwall. Over coffee we talked about the traditional foods that are associated with Christmas, and the conversation meandered to the other festivals that used to be part of the yearly round for our ancestors. As we speculated on the foods that might have gone with those lost celebrations, Jenni said, 'Well, there's your book, then!' But it wasn't a book then, it started out as a blog, 'Feasts and Festivals', where I explored past festivities and old traditions and then cooked something I thought appropriate. Not only was the blog an unexpected success, the research became ever more addictive, and it was that research which led to the book that you hold in your hands.

I need to say at the outset that this is a very personal take on Cornish feasts and festivals. Yes, it contains accounts of festivities that are still very much alive, but it also harks back to some traditions that, for better or worse, are no more. You are unlikely to see people 'trigging' in Mount's Bay or milkmaids dancing through the streets of Truro, but you can

definitely see the Hal an Tow pageant, and if you seek them out, you might find a wassailer or two. The book contains some traditional Cornish recipes, but I've also added other dishes that use the wonderful produce to be found in Cornwall, or which seemed somehow or other to fit the occasion.

I took all the photographs in the book myself with my very modest digital camera, often running round the house holding both it and a plate of hot food in order to catch the best light. Everything you see was photographed as soon as it was ready and then it was eaten, every drop, slice and crumb.

From the time that this book was conceived, many people have been incredibly helpful and supportive. Annabelle Read and Alex Higlett from the Morrab Library in Penzance encouraged me from the very beginning, squirreling out wonderful nuggets of information and eating lots of cake! Library members such as Dr Eric Richards, Cedric Appleby and Glyn Richards have been generous with their own research and with their anecdotes. Many friends have eaten their way through the food I've cooked, and made helpful suggestions. You know who you are – thank you. My husband Tony has, as always, encouraged me do things better than I thought I could. I owe particular thanks to Yvonne Bristow for casting a professional editor's eye over the recipes, and to Alison Hodge for her patience and professionalism. Finally, but definitely not least, I should like to thank Freya Laughton for the quirky and delightful illustrations which bring the whole project to life. Any errors and omissions are, of course, my very own.

Liz Woods, 2013

Notes for the Cook

The recipes usually say full-fat milk, which is what I use. You can substitute semi-skimmed, but you won't get the same creaminess.

I've also specified Cornish sea salt, which comes in fine and coarse grades. The fine is preferable where you are adding salt to dry ingredients rather than liquid ones.

All ovens vary. Temperatures are in degrees Centigrade for conventional electric ovens. For those with fan or gas ovens, this table gives useful equivalent temperatures.

Oven temperatures
130°C/fan 150°C/300°F/gas 2
140°C/fan 160°C/325°F/gas 3
170°C/fan 190°C°/375°F/gas 5
180°C/fan 200°C/400°F/gas 6
200°C/fan 220°C/425°F/gas 7
230°C/fan 250°C/475°F/gas 9

When it comes to measuring ingredients, the recipes are metric throughout. If you prefer to use imperial measurements, here is a list of equivalents. Always use either metric or imperial – never mix them.

Metric/imperial
125 ml	1/4 pint
250 ml	1/2 pint
300 ml	about 2/3 pint
500 ml	1 pint
600 ml	1 pint (pudding bowl)
1 litre	2 pints
1.5 litres	3 pints

Weight
5 ml	1 tsp
10 ml	1 dessert spoon
15 ml	1 tbsp
25 g	1 oz
60 g	2 oz
80 g	3 oz
120 g	4 oz
140 g	5 oz
150 g	6 oz
220 g	8 oz
375g	12 oz
440 g	1 lb
1 kg	2 lb
1.5 kg	3 lb

Length
2.5 cm	1 in
15 cm	6 in
25 cm	10 in
30.5 cm	12 in
61 cm	24 in
1 m	39 in

Twelfth Night... 6 January

Making a special cake for Epiphany, the last of the twelve days of Christmas, is a much older tradition than the Christmas cake with which we're all familiar, and putting tokens into the mixture in order to divine what the coming year might bring, was as prevalent in Cornwall as it was everywhere else in Britain. In Cornwall, a Twelfth Day cake contained three tokens: a ring, a thimble and a sixpence. The cake was cut into the same number of pieces as the people present. If you were the lucky person who found the ring, you would be married within the year. The thimble meant you would never marry, and the coin meant you would die rich! You could simply put in a red kidney bean – that's also traditional.

Twelfth Day cake was not the same as the traditional Christmas cake – all of which had to be eaten by Twelfth Night, just as all the greenery that had decorated the house over the twelve days of Christmas had to be removed, lest a ghost should visit the house during the year. Twelfth Day cake was more often yeast raised. Although it might contain fruit, it was always lighter than the dense fruity Christmas cake that would have been made long before Christmas and lovingly fed with the brandy so freely available in Cornwall.

Twelfth Night was a night for telling tales by firelight, and also the last opportunity for guize dancing, as mumming was called in Cornwall. Traditional guize plays were performed, usually featuring St George and the Dragon – the dastardly Moor of folk memory – and all of that meant lots of dressing up and blackening of faces. The following Monday – Plough Monday – was when the farmers' year began again, and then it was all work until Easter, so perhaps it's understandable that Twelfth Night was celebrated so widely.

In practice, any special cake recipe might have been used for Twelfth Day, but as a contrast to a heavy fruit Christmas cake I have chosen a light yeast-raised crown, similar to those made for the same occasion in some parts of France. I've decorated it with jewels of candied fruit and edible gold powder to represent the gifts of the Magi, whose visit to the infant Jesus is remembered today.

Twelfth Day cake

You will need:

- 250 ml full-fat milk
- 2 medium eggs
- 150 g melted, cooled unsalted butter
- 500 g unbleached strong plain flour
- 80 g caster sugar
- 1½ tsp fine Cornish sea salt
- 2½ tsp easy-blend yeast
- tokens (see page 8), or a red kidney bean – a symbolic gesture, easier on the teeth!
- 5 heaped tbsp icing sugar and a little hot water for glacé icing
- 80 g mixed candied fruit – such as coloured cherries, cranberries, chopped pineapple or crystallized ginger, to decorate
- edible gold powder, to decorate

This makes a large cake and serves about 12.

The simplest way to make this dough is in a bread maker – follow the maker's instructions for a brioche and take out the raw dough to make the crown. It's easy by hand too. In a large bowl, mix all the ingredients together (except for your decoration fruit), and then knead for about 10 minutes on a floured board until the dough is soft and elastic. Put the dough back in the bowl and leave it somewhere warm to rise until doubled in size. Knock the dough back and then, on a floured board, form it into a snake about 60 cm long. Form the snake into a circle, stick the ends together with water and put it on a greased or lined baking sheet. Let the crown rise again in a warm place for 45 minutes.

Preheat the oven to 190°C, then bake for 30–35 minutes or until the crown is golden brown and a light tap on the bottom makes a hollow ring.

Let the crown cool before getting down to the fun part of decorating. This is no time for restraint. You can use glacé icing (add hot water in a fine dribble to the icing sugar to make a thin runny paste), glacé cherries of all colours, candied fruit such as cranberries, chopped pineapple, crystallized ginger and any bits of other glacé fruit you might have left over from Christmas. Edible glitter looks good too – you can get it from specialist cake decorating shops and online.

Don't forget to warn your friends about the tokens!

Twelfth Day cake

St Hilary's Day... 13 January

The church in the village of St Hilary, near Marazion, is dedicated to Saint Hilary, a fourth-century bishop. St Hilary's Day is traditionally supposed to be the coldest day of the year. On this day in 1205 the River Thames froze right over and caused alehouses to sell their beer in chunks by weight rather than by volume. Weather records show that many of the 'big freezes' in British history have started around the middle of January.

The village is in a windy spot overlooking Mount's Bay, and the church's staunch spire stands as a sea-marker that has been used for centuries by sailors, periodically being whitewashed to make it stand out even further. There has been a place of worship here since before 1178, but on Good Friday 1853, a devastating fire destroyed the fifteenth-century church and only the spire was left standing. The church was rebuilt in a simple, Early English style and is now beautifully weathered and looks much older than it actually is.

St Hilary church is well known in Cornwall for its lovely wooden panels of saints that were painted in the 1920s by members of the Newlyn School of Artists, in particular Ernest and Dod Proctor. Dod Proctor also modelled for the stylish image of Joan of Arc which is in the church, and was painted by Annie Walke (1888–1965), the artist wife of the vicar of that time, the controversial and bohemian Father Bernard Walke, a high Anglo-Catholic with strong socialist and pacifist connections. His outspoken and practical support for conscientious objectors in the First World War earned him much criticism, as did his support for those suffering famine in post-revolutionary Russia. The friend of artists and freethinkers, including George Bernard Shaw, Bernard Walke was a figure who was respected and reviled in equal measure.

Despite being loved by the ordinary working people of St Hilary, Father Walke's so-called 'idolatrous practices' and the artistic adornments at St Hilary were the cause of much protest by extreme Protestant agitators from elsewhere. The discontent eventually turned to violence when an armed mob of 50 people from 'up country' entered the church with axes and hammers and smashed the medieval high altar and all the internal

fittings and ornaments. The church was virtually ruined inside. It sounds like something that might have been done by Cromwell's soldiers but it actually happened in 1932. After Father Walke's death in 1937, the church remained in a sad condition for many years, but in the early 1970s it was beautifully restored and the richly coloured and glowing Newlyn School paintings are there for all to see.

Whole cauliflower soup with smoked paprika oil

Whole cauliflower soup with smoked paprika oil

You will need:

- I large onion, peeled and finely chopped
- I clove garlic, peeled and finely chopped
- a knob of butter – about I tbsp
- I medium cauliflower with its leaves and stalks (about I kg), washed
- I medium potato, peeled and chopped into small chunks
- ½ tsp English mustard powder
- I I light chicken or vegetable stock (a cube is fine)
- Cornish sea salt and freshly ground black pepper
- nutmeg
- 2 tbsp olive oil
- I tsp hot smoked paprika, to decorate

This serves about 4.

In January, the sloping fields around St Hilary are full of cauliflowers (known locally as broccoli!) and the harvest is in full swing, so a hot soup for a very cold day seems appropriate. I always steam my cauliflower with a few outside leaves, which I think give it a better flavour, but this recipe goes even further and uses the whole of this underrated vegetable. The spicy hit of the paprika oil really complements this delicious soup.

Sweat the onion and garlic gently in the butter in a large saucepan until soft and translucent but not brown. Roughly chop the cauliflower and leaves, thinly slice the stalks crossways and add it all to the onion with the potato and the mustard powder. Pour over the stock, bring to the boil then cover and simmer for about 25 minutes until the stalks and the potato are soft. Blitz the soup in a food processor or liquidizer until smooth and creamy. Return to the pan, taste, reheat gently and add salt, pepper and a grating of nutmeg.

In a small pan, heat the olive oil then add the paprika and simmer for about 20 seconds – don't burn it! Serve the soup in hot bowls with a dribble of the flavoured oil in the centre.

Shrove Tuesday

In Cornwall, the Monday evening before Shrove Tuesday used to be called nicky-nan-night, and was an excuse for youngsters to roam the streets, rattling doorknobs and running away before angry householders could catch them. A similar custom existed in Brittany where it was called *ninc-kyn-nan-neuf*. There have been many centuries of trade between Cornwall and Brittany, so did Cornish fishermen take our tradition to Brittany, or did the Breton sailors bring it to Cornwall? Or maybe both traditions were survivors of a long-lost and more widespread practice. Who knows?

These days, we tend to think of Shrove Tuesday as just being about pancakes – traditionally a way of eating up leftovers before the start of the Lenten fast. However, Miss Courtney (1834–1920) in her book *Cornish Feasts and Folk Lore* (1890) tells us that there were lots of other goings-on on that day. This is what she has to say about Penzance:

Large quantities of limpets and periwinkles are gathered in the afternoon by the poor people to be cooked for their supper. This is called 'going a-trigging'.

Later in the day, young boys blackened their faces with soot and lay in wait for innocent passers-by, who would then be roughly manhandled and smeared with dirty, greasy hands – not a good night to be out on the streets! If surprising their unwary neighbours wasn't enough, shells and other remains from the shellfish feast were then thrown at doors and windows. Fortunately, Shrove Tuesday was also the time when all the hoses of the local fire brigade were tested – so hopefully the streets were washed clean!

In the east of Cornwall, where perhaps people were more devout and less raucous, Shrove Tuesday was a time when a straw man called Jack o' Lent was made and dressed in old clothes. Representing Judas Iscariot, this scarecrow was paraded through the streets and burned or hanged in effigy to mark the beginning of the Lenten season.

Penzance seafood pancakes

You will need

For the pancake batter:

- 120 g plain flour
- Cornish sea salt
- 2 eggs
- 60 g melted butter
- 250 ml full-fat milk
- handful mixed soft green herbs – (wild garlic leaves or chives, parsley, French tarragon, dill, fennel), finely chopped
- 60 g butter for frying – clarified is best

For the filling:

- 2 cloves garlic, peeled and finely chopped
- 2 tbsp olive oil
- finger-long piece of orange rind
- 2 bay leaves
- 1 tsp dried thyme
- 1 small glass dry white wine
- 400 g tin chopped tomatoes
- 100 g button mushrooms (optional), chopped in half
- 250 ml fish stock (a cube is fine)
- 220 g mixed cooked seafood – scallops, prawns, mussels
- Cornish sea salt, freshly ground pepper
- Bay leaves, to decorate

This makes 6 pancakes.

Shrove Tuesday seems the ideal time to make savoury pancakes with a seafood filling. This recipe has a number of stages, but it's easy to do over the course of the day and the sauce freezes well. We'll start with a green pancake mix. Make the pancakes as thin as you dare.

Batter: Put all the basic ingredients into a liquidizer (hold back a couple of spoonfuls of milk) and blitz them before adding the rest of the milk, if need be. The batter should be the consistency of thin cream. Pour it into a jug and stir in a generous handful of very finely chopped fresh herbs. Let the mixture stand for at least 30 minutes.

Filling: Sauté the garlic in the oil with orange peel and herbs until soft but not brown. Add the wine and boil to reduce for a couple of minutes. Add tomatoes, stock, and mushrooms if using. Season. Simmer in an open pan until the sauce is thick and chunky – about 20 minutes. You can now set the filling aside. When you're ready, add the cooked seafood.

Melt some butter and skim off the milky solids to clarify and use this to grease your pancake pan. Make the pancakes in the usual way and layer them between sheets of baking

Penzance seafood pancakes

paper while you use up all the batter. When they are cool, put a couple of tablespoons of the seafood sauce on each one and roll up.

Preheat the oven to 180°C.

Place the filled pancakes side-by-side, seam-side down, in a buttered gratin dish. Cover with foil, and bake for about 30 minutes or until the sauce is bubbling hot.

Hurling Match at St Columb Major

In the moorland parish of Minions near St Cleer are three circles of standing stones known as The Hurlers. A line drawn through the circle points directly to the Bronze Age burial chamber at Rillaton, in which was found in 1837 a wonderfully decorated Early Bronze Age golden cup now in the British Museum. According to legend, The Hurlers are the bodies of a group of men who played a hurling match on a Sunday and were turned to stone for their sins.

Hurling used to be a common sport in Cornwall. Its origins are lost, but it may have a connection with Irish hurling and with medieval football. Richard Carew (1555–1620), in his classic, *The Survey of Cornwall* (1602), describes seeing a hurling match:

> Whosoever getteth seizure of this ball, findeth himselfe generally pursued by the adverse party; neither will they leave, till he be layd flat on Gods dear earth...
> The Hurlers take their next way over hilles, dales, hedges, ditches; yea, and thorow bushes, briers, mires, plashes and rivers whatsoever; so as you shall sometimes see 20 or 30 lie tugging together in the water, scrambling and scratching for the ball. A play (verily) both rude & rough, and yet such, as is not destitute of policies, in some sort resembling the feats of warre.

Today, only three places in Cornwall hold hurling games – annually in St Ives and St Columb, and once every five years in Bodmin. The game is still played with a ball – about the size of a cricket ball, made of apple wood covered in silver.

Every year there are two hurling matches at St Columb Major, one on Shrove Tuesday and one a week the following Saturday which is even rougher than the first, as the victors of the first game fight to retain ownership of the ball. The ball-throwing game is played between townsmen and countrymen, starting with the cry, 'Town and Country do your best, for in this Parish I must rest.' The opposing teams scramble, fight and elbow for the ball in order to pass it through their goal, one a mile into the country, the other a mile out of the other side of town.

This is a tradition with no organizing committee, no referee, little publicity, very few rules, and which seems to happen almost spontaneously. Anyone can take part, and in the early stages the ball is tossed between all the participants as they run through the town. The game may be slowed down at this stage to allow children and non-players to touch the silver ball for luck and, some say, for fertility. The game starts in the late afternoon and finishes about 8 pm when one lucky player manages to get the ball through his team's goal.

After it's all over, a large number of tired and dirty players head back into town and the ball is taken to the pub where it is dunked in a gallon jug of best beer, which everyone then shares.

Hurling can be a dangerous game, as witnessed by a note in the church-wardens' accounts of St Martin and St Meriadoc Church in Camborne, which says:

1705, William Trevarthen buried in the church, being disstroid to a hurling with Redruth men at the high dounes… .

Heavy cake

Heavy cake

Here's a solid Cornish dish fit for a solid Cornish hurler. Heavy, or *heava*, cake is a traditional Cornish treat also called *fuggan*. *Heava* derives from the cry of the 'huers' who waited on cliff tops and watched for pilchard shoals off shore. The cry of 'Hevva! hevva!' signified it was time to rush down to the boats and put to sea. The net pattern on top of the cake is very traditional. There are lots of variations; this one is based on a recipe in *Cornish Recipes: Ancient and Modern* (1929), and from the recollections of a number of Newlyn ladies.

Heavy cake should be shaley on top and just slightly squidgy in the middle. It's best eaten warm from the oven with a strong cup of tea.

In a bowl, rub the flour and fats together until the mixture is like fine breadcrumbs, then add 2 tsp sugar, salt, lemon rind and the fruit. Gradually stir in enough milk to make a soft but not sticky dough. Turn out on to a floured board and with a rolling pin, form it into an oval shape about 2 cm thick and 24 cm wide, then roll it up like a Swiss roll and set aside for an hour or two.

Preheat the oven to 200°C.

Now roll out the dough again into an oval and use a sharp knife to mark the top in a diamond pattern. Brush with egg and sprinkle with sugar.

Put on a greased baking tray and bake for about 20–25 minutes until lightly golden and cooked through. Cut into rectangular slices to serve.

St Piran's Day... 5 March

As with many Celtic saints, the life of the sixth-century St Piran is a mix of hazy memory, dubious fact and active imagination. Whether St Piran was also St Ciaran of Ireland we really don't know, but we do know that the cult of St Piran began in Perranzabuloe in the tenth century, and the earliest St Piran's chapel, now buried in Perran Sands, dates from that time. St Piran is also the saint of the parish churches of Perranarworthal and Perranuthnoe, where there was a guild of St Piran in 1457.

St Piran is the patron saint of tinners, and of Cornwall. His feast day was a traditional holiday for Cornish miners, and parades by tinners showing off the saint's relics or emblems were an early feature of the day across the county. The Cost Book of Great Work Mine near Breage shows that in the mid-eighteenth century, every man and boy working there was paid an 'allowance for Perrantide'.

St Piran's flag, the standard of Cornwall, is a white cross on a black background, symbolizing the triumph of good over evil and the tin metal trapped in the ore. There are still St Piran's Day processions all over Cornwall, and the flag flies valiantly over them all.

Cornish pasties

To celebrate St Piran's Day, there is really no alternative – it has to be a pasty. You can buy a very decent pasty in every town in Cornwall, but nothing beats a home-baked one.

Let's deal with all the pasty myths first. The Cornish pasty developed as portable, hot and sustaining food for a tin miner. Made in the morning (or more likely baked overnight in the bread oven), its pastry case would keep the contents warm until time for croust, as the meal break underground was called. The disposable pastry crimp around the edge meant a man could eat his pasty with dirty hands and the pastry should be resilient enough to take down the mine in the pocket of a working jacket. This is not the time for delicate, fragile pastry – a pasty crust should be substantial.

In the early days, the crust would have been made with coarse barley flour, but I find a little wholemeal spelt flour added to the mixture adds a homely texture and taste.

These days the filling is beef – usually skirt – with potato, onion and swede, butter and lots of seasoning, nothing else. In earlier times the filling might have been whatever came to hand – it could have been rabbit, vegetables, offal or pilchards. It used to be said that the devil wouldn't dare enter Cornwall in case he got baked into a pasty, which suggests that anything and everything might end up wrapped in crust and baked!

'Crimp at the top' or 'crimp at the side' is the big decision. Crimp at the side is the West Cornwall way, so that's what I do, and I think it's easier to eat – with your fingers and a cup of sweet tea.

Cornish pasty

Cornish pasties

You will need:

- shortcrust pastry, made with 120 g butter, 140 g lard, 375 g plain flour, 120 g spelt flour, 5–6 tbsp water, a good pinch of fine Cornish sea salt
- 150 g swede, peeled
- 2 medium potatoes, peeled
- 2 onions, peeled
- 400 g beef skirt
- Cornish sea salt and freshly ground black pepper
- a knob of butter for each pasty
- 1 egg, beaten, to glaze

This makes 6 pasties.

Roll out the pastry and cut out six circles about 18 cm diameter. I use a small plate to make them all the same size.

Chop the onions, swede and potatoes into fingernail-sized pieces. Put into three separate bowls, and cover the potato with water to stop it going black.

Chop the meat into very small pieces across the grain – that's important, to keep the meat chunky – and put them into a fourth bowl. Now you can get a production line going.

Preheat the oven to 200°C.

Put a good pile of onion, swede, meat and potato, in that order, on to each pastry circle and season generously with salt and black pepper. Remember the contents will shrink as the pasty cooks, so fill it well. Pop a knob of butter on the top, and brush around the edge of your circle with a little water. Fold the pastry over from front to back and press down the edge. Make sure it doesn't leak by turning and twisting the pastry edge. This is the all-important 'crimp'. Brush the pasties with egg, put them on a baking tray and bake them for 25 minutes, then reduce the heat to 170°C for another 40 minutes.

Note: It is traditional to mark each pasty with initials to denote whose is which. The initials can either be pricked in the pastry with a skewer or made from the scraps of paste left over and stuck on. This way, each pasty can be tailored to the taste of different members of the family.

Good Friday

Good Friday has become synonymous with hot cross buns, but few of us know their fascinating history. Spiced yeast buns became very popular in Tudor times, and for a long while bakers were restricted as to when they could make them. Here's what the Clerk of the London Markets said in 1592:

> That no bakers at any times make or sell by retail within or without their houses unto any of the Queen's subjects any spice cakes, buns, biscuits or other spice bread… except it be for burials, or on Friday before Easter, or at Christmas, upon pain of forfeiture of all such spiced bread to the poor.

> Elizabeth David, *English Bread and Yeast Cookery* (1977)

That didn't prevent such breads being made in the home. By the time of James I, the law, which in any case had more to do with suppressing Popery than regulating bakers, had been relaxed. Two hundred years later, nineteenth-century researchers into British folklore discovered the widespread superstition that yeast products baked on Good Friday never went mouldy and were capable of working miracles.

These marvelous breads had to be marked with the sign of the cross, and numerous customs were associated with them. The bread might be buried in a wheat field to ensure a good harvest, or thrown into a river to prevent floods. Good Friday bread was taken by sailors as a charm against shipwreck and kept in the house to protect it against fire. It was also kept and crumbled into the food of sick animals, and no doubt sick people too.

Scholars have speculated that hot cross buns are a last remnant of a spring festival involving extinguishing all the lights and fires on Easter Eve and lighting them afresh the next day from a new source. This was a ritual of renewal practised across many cultures in spring, and in the Christian tradition it is dramatically enhanced by being performed in a darkened church. Many churchwardens' account books record the purchase of materials for this rite, and parish households used the flames kindled thereby to restart the domestic hearth fires deliberately extinguished the evening before.

In Cornwall, spiced buns are made with that most exotic and expensive of spices – saffron. Popular folklore says that the Phoenicians brought saffron to Cornwall and traded it for tin. A more hard-headed interpretation is that when saffron fell out of use in the rest of Britain in the late Middle Ages, it continued to be used in Cornwall. It certainly continued to be grown here. According to Cyril Noall, writing in the *Western Morning News* (8 April 1975), in 1841, a piece of land sold in Veryan on the Roseland peninsula was described as 'all that tenement called the saffron parks situate in the parish containing by estimation fourteen acres.'

Saffron hot cross buns

You will need:

- 250 ml milk
- 500 g strong plain flour
- 60 g currants
- 25 g sultanas
- 25g mixed peel
- 1 tsp fine Cornish sea salt
- 60 g light soft brown sugar
- good pinch saffron threads
- 1½ tsp easy-blend yeast
- 60 g butter
- 1 large egg
- 2 tbsp each full-fat milk and light brown sugar for a glaze

This makes 12 buns.

Cornish saffron cake – which is bread not cake, rich with butter, dried fruit and heady spice – was traditionally made at Easter, for parish feasts, and at Christmas, when each roll was given a little 'topknot'. You can buy saffron cake all the year round now, but for special occasions it's lovely to make at home, and fills the house with a delicious aroma.

Warm 250 ml milk in a pan to blood heat. Off the heat put in the saffron threads to in-fuse, for about 20 minutes. Mix together the flour, salt, sugar and yeast in a bowl. Melt the butter until liquid but not hot. Whisk the egg and add the saffron milk and melted butter. Pour into the dry ingredients and mix well, then add the fruit. Knead on a floured board until smooth. Leave to rise in a warm place until doubled in size – about an hour.

When well risen divide into two, then two again, and again until you have twelve pieces of dough each about the size of a golf ball.

With the palm of your hand on the top of the dough, shape each bun by rolling it on your floured board until it is a perfect sphere. Put on a baking tray. Make a cross on the top of each bun using a very sharp knife or the tines of a fork. If you prefer, roll out very thin bits of dough and lay them at right angles over the buns. Cover and leave to rise again in a warm place for about 30 minutes until well risen and puffy.

Preheat the oven to 190°C.

Bake for 15–20 minutes until lightly golden.

Meanwhile, make the glaze by boiling together 2 tbsp each milk and light brown sugar until bubbly and syrupy. Paint this on the buns

Saffron hot cross buns

while still hot. Do this twice, so they will be conker-like in their brown shininess. If you are short of time, simply dust them with icing sugar, as above.

Trevithick Day in Camborne... April

Going up Camborne Hill, coming down
Going up Camborne Hill, coming down
The horses stood still;
The wheels went around;
Going up Camborne Hill coming down.

On Christmas Eve 1801, two young cousins and their friends rode the first ever, full-sized steam locomotive carriage up Camborne Hill. Three days later, the first locomotive carriage accident occurred when the driver, Andrew Vivian, Richard Trevithick's cousin, lost control of the vehicle and ended up in a ditch. A contemporary eye witness recorded that 'the parties adjourned to the hotel and comforted their hearts with roast goose and proper drinks'. Unfortunately, they forgot to put out the fire under the boiler, which boiled dry, caught fire and destroyed the whole contraption. The story is a leitmotif of Trevithick's amazing life, boundless enthusiasm, great gifts, hard work and triumph, all followed by total disaster.

The event is commemorated in the famous Cornish folk song *Going up Camborne Hill, coming down!* – often sung at Cornish rugby matches and poignantly sung by Rick Rescorla from Hayle as he heroically helped people escape from New York's Twin Towers on 11 September 2001.

Richard Trevithick (1771–1833) was born in the parish of Illogan, the heart of Cornwall's mining district. His father was a mine captain (manager), and he showed engineering promise from an early age. At nineteen, he was acting as a consultant on mine engines all over the county. He went on to invent and patent many engineering devices that hugely increased the profitability of mines in Cornwall and as far afield as Peru and Costa Rica. But financial success evaded him, and he died poor and alone in a London hotel. The gold watch he had brought back from South America was sold to pay for his funeral.

Since his death, Trevithick's huge contribution to the industrial revolution has been recognized. Every April, Camborne holds a 'Trevithick Day', when steam enthusiasts from all over the country bring their engines to town. It's a great day – noisy, smelly, steamy, of course – and lots of fun.

Spotted Dick

The administrative centre of a Cornish mine was the count house, where the mine captain had his office, meetings took place, investors were entertained and miners paid. In charge of the kitchen was the count house cook – hugely important to the wellbeing of the mine. This lady cooked boiled beef and vegetables in a deep iron cauldron for the mine captain, his visitors and the 'adventurers', as investors were known. After the beef, over her open hearth, she would steam a suet pudding. So here is… Spotted Dick!

Mix together all the dry ingredients, then add the egg, milk and orange rind and juice. You should have a soft batter that drops off a spoon, so add a little more milk if necessary. Grease a pudding bowl and place two long strips of baking parchment about 2 cm wide at right angles in the bottom of the bowl; they should be long enough to hang over the edges.

Cut a circle of baking parchment or kitchen foil larger than the diameter of the bowl and make a pleat in it (so the pudding can expand in cooking). Spoon the pudding mixture into the bowl, fold over the parchment and tie it on with string around the edge of the bowl.

Put the pudding into a steamer if you have one, or a lidded saucepan with a heat-proof trivet to lift it from the base of the pan. Add hot water to about half way up the pudding and steam for about 2 hours. Remove from the steamer and turn the pudding out of the bowl on to a warmed plate, using the strips to help you. Serve hot with custard.

This pudding reheats well in a microwave. I sometimes make it with dried cranberries instead of currants around Christmas time.

Spotted Dick

May Day

The Anglo Saxons called May Ðrimilcemonað – 'month of three milkings'. The lush grass of early summer led to an abundance of creamy milk ready to turn into clotted cream or cheese. It is hard to underestimate the importance of milk to our ancestors. It was fresh, on the spot, preservable protein.

The farm dairy was traditionally a woman's preserve, and dairymaids supposedly had wonderful complexions. This was probably true, not because they washed their faces in May dew, but because, as Edward Jenner discovered, they were immune to smallpox and had ready access to fresh, nutritious food.

May Day was a holiday for milkmaids, who dressed in their best and danced through the streets with a May garland of polished metal utensils balanced on the head of a male friend. Samuel Pepys walked to Westminster on the morning of 1 May 1667 'meeting many milkmaids with their garlands among their pails, dancing with a fiddler before them'.

St Mary's on the Isles of Scilly is one place where May Day traditions still survive. The children of the island, dressed in white, sing May tunes, decorate the path of the May Queen, and then dance around the maypole. The white dresses and lovely island flowers make it a beautiful and memorable occasion.

In *Cornish Feasts and Folk Lore*, Miss Courtney tells us that:

> Boys and girls in Cornwall sat up until 12 o'clock on the eve of May Day and then marched around the towns and villages with musical instruments collecting their friends and going a-Maying. May Day is ushered in at Penzance by the discordant blowing of tin horns.

Penzance youngsters would also blow on May Day whistles – little tubes of green wood, usually sycamore, whittled especially for the occasion by a fond father or grandfather – a custom still remembered by many older people in the town. On May Day morning, young people used to call on their neighbours with boughs of hawthorn to decorate doorways, and then to demand a treat of freshly clotted cream, junket or syllabub – 'suck cream', as it was often called in Cornwall.

Syllabub

You will need:
- grated rind of 1 unwaxed lemon
- 100 ml (small glass) medium sweet white wine or sherry
- 2 tbsp brandy
- 2 heaped tbsp icing sugar
- 250 ml double cream
- pinch freshly grated nutmeg
- 4 small sprigs rosemary, to decorate

This serves 4.

There's a long and well-established tradition in relation to syllabub. You are supposed to make it by squirting the milk straight from the cow and then whisking it with a rosemary twig. I suggest using an electric whisk, unless you really want to creep out on a May morning with your milking stool.

Most old Cornish receipt books have a recipe for syllabub which often contained brandy – plentiful and cheap, and usually from a barrel that had somehow by-passed the Customs Officer. Here's a 1791 example using cider:

Sweeten a quart of cider with refined sugar, grate a nutmeg over it; and milk the cow into your liquor. When you have added what is necessary pour in half a pint of the sweetest cream.

And here's a more modern version. If you have to leave this before serving you may need to re-whisk to keep the soft, pillowy bulk that you are looking for.

Add the lemon rind to the wine and brandy in a bowl, add the icing sugar and leave to steep for at least an hour. Strain the alcohol into a jug. Whisk the cream in a large bowl, and as it thickens gradually add the sweetened alcohol. Add the grated nutmeg. Chill before serving, and spoon into chilled glasses, or a dish as here, at the last minute. Add the rosemary to decorate.

Syllabub

Padstow 'Obby 'Oss… May Day

There is some controversy about the origins of Padstow 'Obby 'Oss Festival. The first written account of it was in 1803; it was not mentioned by sixteenth- and seventeenth-century travellers to Cornwall, who delighted in the remnants of ancient folk practices still found there. So it seems likely that the Padstow 'Oss was born sometime in the 1700s.

Hobby-horses date back much further, and were essential to mumming celebrations in the Middle Ages. The first mention of such a hobby-horse in Cornwall is in a mystery play about the life of St Meriadoc, which was performed in and around Camborne in the late-fifteenth century. Like many similar folk practices, hobby-horses were banned by the Puritans during the seventeenth century. Maybe the Padstow 'Oss was resurrected with the restoration of the monarchy in 1660, but we simply don't know.

May Day begins in Padstow to the sound of massed unaccompanied voices heralding the start of summer, and the town fills with locals and tourists who come for the 'Obby 'Oss processions. There are, in fact, two 'osses – the 'Old Red 'Oss' and the 'Blue Ribbon'. Each is portrayed by a man in a voluminous black, hooped garment wearing a frightening, stylized horse mask. The 'osses emerge from their different stables early in the day, accompanied by a retinue of 'Mayers' or 'Teasers' dressed in white shirts and blue or red sashes, depending on which horse they are following. There's lots of noise and music from accordions and drums as the 'osses process and, of course, there is singing:

Unite unite and let us all unite, for summer is acome unto day.

The 'osses behave in a provocative fashion as they parade through the streets, often darting off if they see a pretty girl or someone looking a bit scared. The crowd gets very excited and the whole thing is a joyful celebration of the beginning of summer.

Mussels in saffron cream

You will need:

- 1 kg mussels in the shell (buying them ready cleaned and vacuum-packed avoids tedious preparation)
- 80 g unsalted butter
- 1 shallot, peeled and finely chopped
- 100 ml (small glass) dry white wine
- good pinch saffron strands
- 100 ml Cornish clotted cream
- finely chopped parsley and lemon pieces, to garnish (optional)
- Cornish sea salt and freshly ground black pepper

This serves 2.

These days, Padstow is one of the foodie towns of Cornwall, so I've chosen a recipe to suit. It is taken from a copy of the now defunct magazine, *Cornish Scene*. In the 1980s, contributors often sent in articles to the magazine under pseudonyms to hide their identity. This recipe was sent in by someone calling himself Moonward Rickshine. Who was that? Thank you anyway, whoever you are.

Rinse the mussels in cold water and discard any that don't close when tapped smartly with the back of a knife. Melt the butter in a large pan and cook the finely chopped shallot until softened and slightly coloured. Pour in the wine and let it bubble for two minutes. Add the mussels, put the lid on tight and steam the mussels for a few minutes, just until they open. Discard any that don't open.

Lift the mussels from the pan and set aside. Use a sieve to strain the liquid into a bowl and add the saffron. Return to the pan and simmer over a steady heat until the liquid is reduced by two-thirds. Add the cream and reheat gently, then taste and season. Return the mussels to the sauce to reheat, and sprinkle with parsley before serving in deep, warmed bowls. Garnish with lemon quarters, if liked.

Mussels in saffron cream

Helston Flora Day... May

And soon I heard such a bustling and
   prancing,
And then I saw the whole village were
   dancing,
In and out of the houses they came,
Old folk, young folk, all the same,
In that quaint old Cornish town.
                    The Floral Dance, by Katie Moss
                                     (1881–1947)

Flora Day in Helston is one of the most traditional Cornish festivals, with an unbroken tradition going back hundreds of years. Helston
is *en fête* on Flora Day, the streets decorated with greenery, bluebells and branches.
Bunches of lily-of-the-valley are placed in
windows and everyone dresses in their best.
The town is thronged with people; bands
play, and dances take place through the
streets and in an out of the yards and houses,
to the familiar tune of The Furry Dance.

   The word 'furry' is usually reckoned to
come from an old Celtic word, *feur*, meaning 'festivity', but it might also be connected
with the Cornish word *gwyr*, meaning 'grass',
and, by association, 'green'. There were once
other dances and days of this kind elsewhere
in Cornwall and, no doubt, in the rest of the
British Isles, but only the Helston Flora sur-
vives, its beginnings now completely obscure.

   One of the major features of the day is the
Hal-an-Tow pageant, banned as too raucous
by the Victorians, but revived in the 1930s.
This involves the cutting of sycamore branches to celebrate the spring and the singing of
the Hal-an-Tow song 'For Summer is a come
O, and the Winter is a Gone O'. People
dress in the clothes of the greenwood and
process through the streets singing.

   Despite the crowds and all the pushing and
pressing to get a good view, I love Flora Day.
The main dance, with the ladies in evening
gowns and the men smartened up is just lovely, and it's real – 'really real', if you see what
I mean. It's done for tradition and community and fun, not for tourists, although tourists there are aplenty. It's not self-consciously
reinvented, it just is. Go if you get the chance.

   And there's loads of delicious food and
drink in Helston on Flora Day, from pasties,
saffron cakes and ice cream, to pints of Spin-
go – a beer unique to Helston's Blue Anchor.

Wild herb tart

You will need:

- 375 g shortcrust pastry
- 220 g full-fat cream cheese
- 2 large eggs
- 100 ml full-fat milk
- a big handful of wild herbs or mixed leaves, washed and finely chopped
- ½ tsp ground mace or nutmeg
- Cornish sea salt and freshly ground black pepper
- 22-cm flan dish

This serves 6.

I'm sure that in years gone by thrifty Cornish housewives didn't hesitate to take their baskets and go foraging for the pot. This delicious and simple tart uses that most common of Cornish spring weeds – the three-cornered leek. It's usually referred to as 'wild garlic' in the South West, and is the scourge of gardeners. However, making it into this delightful tart does feel like getting one's own back. I like to use mixed herbs such as wild garlic, nettle tops, sorrel and wild fennel, but in the absence of wild leaves, finely chopped spinach, chives and parsley would do very well. Cornish new potatoes and a leafy salad make good accompaniments.

Preheat the oven to 200°C.

Roll out the pastry and line a flan dish. Bake the empty pastry case for 15 minutes (you may need to support the sides with baking paper or foil). Mix the eggs, cream cheese and milk until smooth, then add the chopped herbs and the mace or nutmeg. Season well.

Put the tart on a baking tray, pour on the egg and herb mixture and place in the oven. Bake for about 25 minutes until golden brown. Serve lukewarm.

Wild herb tart

Beating the Parish Bounds on Rogation Day

The origins of a formal occasion when parishioners walk together with sticks or willow wands, swishing at the boundaries of their parish, are very ancient, and despite it being a Church event, its origins are definitely non-Christian. In the past, Beating the Bounds was usually associated with Rogation Sunday, the fifth Sunday after Easter, but nowadays it might be done at any time in the summer.

Beating the Bounds takes place in a number of parishes across Cornwall at different times. It's worth looking out for, so you can participate in one of the oldest traditions still practised in Britain. Bodmin, Truro, St Ives and Liskeard all have their boundary traditions. Check out other parishes too, because some towns and villages process only to mark important national or local events, such as royal jubilees and parish anniversaries.

Rogation processions most likely developed from the very similar Roman practice of Ambarvalia, carried out during the Roman occupation of Britain, when the local priest and his flock processed around the fields of a given area, praying for a good harvest. When the bounds of St Ives are beaten, the harvest of the sea is incorporated into the blessing. Local tradition tells us that in Breock, where part of the parish boundary is water, boats had to be used to get around!

Beating the Bounds also had a practical use in a time before maps, reminding parishioners where the boundaries of a parish were and who owned the land within it. The poet and critic Geoffrey Grigson (1905–85), who came from Pelynt near Looe, wrote a book about his home village called *Freedom of the Parish* (1954). In it he says:

> I feel that extraordinary magnetism coming to me, for example, from a meadow on the boundaries of the manor of Pelynt and the manor of Trelawne where the tenants of the two were constantly in dispute, nearly seven centuries ago, over the use of a spring into which I can still dip my fingers.

Elderflower cordial

You will need:
- 20–30 young elderflower heads
- 1 l water
- 1 kg caster sugar
- 2 lemons, washed and thinly sliced
- 60 g citric acid (obtainable from wine-making suppliers)
- several bottles with stoppers

This makes just over 1 litre of cordial.

Rogation Days were 'grass days', when no meat or fish could be eaten, and the parish walks would often end with an outdoor celebration of cake and 'gang ale'. Such walks were sometimes called 'gang days' from the Anglo Saxon word *gangen*, meaning 'to go'.

I love the idea of a Rammalation feast – the name must be a rural corruption of 'perambulation', and 'gang ale' signifies not a particular kind of ale, but one made for the occasion of the 'ganging'. However, since Rogation Sunday coincides with the Cornish countryside being at its most beautiful, I thought elderflower cordial might be more appropriate.

Pick the elderflower heads when they are still young. They smell very catty when they start to go over, so you need the heads when they still have some unopened florets.

Take the elderflowers home and rinse them very well; you don't need to pull the petals away from the little stalks, although I do remove the thick stalk that holds the flower head together.

Put the water and sugar in a pan and heat gently until the sugar has dissolved. Add the lemon slices, citric acid and elderflowers. Set aside for 24 hours and then strain into sterilized bottles and keep in the fridge.

Dilute with iced fizzy water and serve with a slice of lemon. This is also a very good addition to stewed gooseberries.

Elderflower cordial

Bugle Band Contest... 18 June

A band festival at a place called Bugle – what could be more appropriate? The proper title of the Bugle Band Contest is The West of England Bandsman's Festival, and apart from a couple of short breaks during times of war, it has been held at Bugle near St Austell since 1912. Mollinis Park rings out to the harmonies and oom-pah-pahs of dozens of brass and silver bands that come to Bugle from across the West Country. It's a grand day out for bandspeople and music lovers.

In the nineteenth century, brass bands sprang up across Cornwall as they did in the north of England, associated with mines, factories and other works. Band contests provided an opportunity to show off the bands' skills, earn a few pennies and take a much-needed respite from harsh working conditions.

Bugle village is deep in china clay country, and when the band contest was established, the industry was producing around a million tons of china clay every year, not just for ceramics but also for kaolin's lesser-known use in the manufacture of quality paper.

Cornish china clay was discovered in 1746 by William Cookworthy (1705–80), a Quaker apothecary and polymath who later patented its use for his porcelain factory in Plymouth. The industrial villages around St Austell grew up around the china clay industry.

There are still huge deposits of kaolin around Bugle, but they are now under-exploited and the industry has significantly declined. Ironically, it is The Eden Project, with its huge biomes, constructed in a disused china clay pit, which has become the most popular tourist destination in Cornwall, bringing renewed prosperity to the area.

Less than twenty miles from Bugle is the Tregothnan Estate. It is believed that, not long after William Cookworthy started producing porcelain from Cornish china clay, Tregothnan became the first place in Britain to grow camellias outdoors. *Camellia sinensis* – the Chinese camellia, more commonly known as tea – is now grown commercially at Tregothnan, and Cornish tea can be bought across the county, so it seems appropriate to use it to make a tea bread and serve it on a Victorian porcelain plate that may or may not have been made using Cornish china clay.

Cornish tea bread

This loaf improves after a day or so. You can, of course, make it with any black tea – it is particularly delicious made with black vanilla tea or Earl Grey. Serve thinly sliced and heavily buttered.

Put the fruit, sugar, marmalade and hot tea in a bowl and leave overnight until cold. If time is short, you can speed up the process by bringing the whole thing to the boil then simmering for no more than 5 minutes.

Preheat the oven to 160°C.

Add the flour, egg and lemon rind to the cold fruit mixture, and stir until thoroughly mixed together. Grease a 440 g loaf tin with butter and line it with baking paper. Bake for about an hour and a half, or until a light tap on the bottom makes a hollow ring.

Cornish tea bread

Golowan... June

The custom of lighting bonfires at the summer solstice, which coincides with the Feast of St John the Baptist, towards the end of June, is a tradition that stretches way back into our pagan past. In the nineteenth century, British folklorists found lots of examples of midsummer rites. William Borlase (1696–1772), Vicar of Ludgvan, in his *Antiquities of Cornwall* (1754), described the midsummer fires of Cornwall in some detail:

> In Cornwall the Festival Fires called
> Bonfires are kindled on the eve of St John
> the Baptist... and midsummer is thence in
> the Cornish tongue called 'Golvan' which
> signifies both light and rejoicing.

St John's Day celebrates the fullness of the year, marking the turning point towards harvest and shorter days. St John's Eve was once also auspicious for the collection of herbs and the making of potions and simples (medicines made from one plant). Churches were decorated with birch twigs and fennel, and plays, processions and pageants were common.

Because the midsummer fires smacked of both Catholic religious fervour and pagan rites, they fell foul of the Reformation, but some remote places held on to their midsummer bonfire tradition. One of these was the most western tip of the mainland – West Cornwall. Penzance was still holding midsummer revels well into the 1800s. There is a strong link between Penzance and St John through the Knights Hospitallers, who owned the mother parish of Madron, so perhaps that contributed to keeping the tradition going.

Penzance sits on a short, stumpy headland poking out into Mount's Bay. The St John's Eve tradition was to set fire to what you had most of, and that usually meant old fish barrels filled with tar which were set rolling through the streets, and torches made of tar-soaked canvas were paraded around the town. In the countryside, bonfires were lit on carns and hilltops, and circle dances took place around the embers.

The feast of Golowan, as it was known, eventually foundered in the 1800s. But all was not lost. The Old Cornwall Society revived the bonfire tradition across the peninsula in 1921, and 70 years later, Penzance again began celebrating Golowan, as a week-long community festival culminating on Mazey Day with a fabulous extravaganza of mock mayor electing, produce stalls, fantastic processions with huge puppets, and a wonderful firework display.

The Sunday after Mazey Day is Quay Fair Day, a gentler celebration when you take your sweetheart down to the quayside and promenade along eating strawberries, which used to be sold there on a plate of leaves.

Summer fruit shortcake

Summer fruit shortcakes

You will need:

- 120 g butter
- 150 g plain flour, sifted
- 60 g caster sugar
- pinch fine Cornish sea salt
- grated zest of 1 orange
- a punnet of fat raspberries, ripe cherries or sliced strawberries (tiny wild strawberries are even more heavenly!)
- double cream, whipped until thick, or Cornish clotted cream
- icing sugar

This makes 10 shortcakes.

Quay Fair is still very much part of the Golowan celebrations – so here is a sweet delight.

First make some orange-flavoured shortbread biscuits. I like to use the sort of butter which is specifically sold for baking (check in your supermarket chill cabinet), because it gives a 'shorter' and crisper result. Alternatively, use French or Danish butter, which has a lower moisture content than English butter.

Soften the butter until it is very soft but not liquid. Mix into the flour and salt, then add the sugar and orange zest and mix with a wooden spoon until you have a smooth dough. Chill. Roll out the dough to the thickness of a pound coin and cut into 5–7 cm rounds using a pastry cutter or upturned glass.

Preheat the oven to 150°C.

Bake on an oven tray for 25 minutes, or until a very light gold. You don't want the shortcakes too brown. Cool on a wire rack.

Sandwich the biscuits together with the cream and the soft fruit. Dredge with icing sugar.

Eat them soon before they go soft.

Bodmin Riding… 2 July

The first weekend in July is Bodmin Heritage Day and Bodmin Riding. It surprises some people to know that Cornwall is not far short of 100 miles long from the border with Devon right down to Land's End. Bodmin Moor is more than half way up, so to reach western Cornwall from the north you have to cross the moor – a place of dark deeds, peat bogs, Jamaica Inn, and haunt of the famous 'Beast of Bodmin', a jaguar-sized black cat, which may or may not be mythical.

Until the coming of the railways, Bodmin was the last outpost of so-called civilization – the assizes were here, the gaol was here, the mental hospital, the barracks and the priory. Beyond Bodmin Moor, the gentry and their authority held little sway, and those living north of the moor believed that in the west of the county, religion was tempered with superstition, there was smuggling and wrecking and the people lived on their wits and on the edge.

Bodmin has a fascinating history. Before the Reformation it was the holiest town in Cornwall, with Bodmin Priory the proud possessor of the bones of the sixth-century St Petroc. At some point the bones were lost (maybe the beast got them), but during Bodmin Riding the ivory casket in which they had been kept is paraded through the town in the sort of procession more usually associated with Catholic towns of southern Europe. The procession was begun by the ancient guilds of Bodmin, and is unusual because it is accompanied by people on horseback – hence 'Bodmin Riding'. A special brew of ale – Riding Ale – is made for the weekend, and on Saturday there is much jollification as the people of Bodmin try to capture 'The Beast'.

Another historical event commemorated during the heritage weekend is the hanging of Nicholas Boyer, a former Mayor of Bodmin who was executed in the town square for his part in the Prayer Book Rebellion of 1549. The enforcement of prayers in English instead of Latin was staunchly resisted in the far west where the Cornish language was still spoken. The failure to translate the Bible and prayer book into Cornish is held by many scholars to be the cause of its demise as the vernacular.

Riding Ale casserole

Riding Ale casserole

To celebrate the heritage of Bodmin, here's a Cornish beef casserole in which the meat is simmered slowly in Cornish ale. I use shin, which I cut myself into bigger chunks than my butcher does; organic ale made by a small local brewery, and rapeseed oil to sauté the meat because it browns it better than olive oil does. For a good, deep flavour, I marinate the beef overnight in the ale, and I think that when cooked, this stew is better kept until the next day then gently reheated.

In winter, you could make dumplings to have with this, or bake it in a puff pastry case. At the end of a chilly summer day, it would be great with crusty bread, followed by a green salad with a sharp dressing.

Marinate the beef overnight in the ale with the herbs and orange peel.

The next day, drain the beef well, set aside the marinade, and pat the meat dry with kitchen paper. Sauté the onions and garlic in 2 tbsp of oil until golden brown, then remove from the pan with a slotted spoon and set aside. Put the meat into a plastic bag with the seasoned flour, shake it about, then sauté it in batches in the rest of the oil (you'll probably need to add more) until brown and crusty.

Preheat the oven to 150° C.

Deglaze the pan with the marinade and put everything into a casserole, adding sufficient beef stock to just cover the meat. Heat the casserole on the hob until it bubbles, cover and put in the oven for 2 hours. Taste and adjust the seasoning before serving.

The Knill Ceremony at St Ives… 25 July

Observant visitors to St Ives will soon spot a conspicuous 15-metre granite obelisk on the summit of Worvas Hill behind the town. Those prepared to make the stiffish climb to the top will see that it is a memorial to John Knill (1733–1811), a former Mayor of St Ives. Knill built the steeple to be his mausoleum, but failing to have the ground properly consecrated, he gave his body to be dissected instead, and what remains of him is actually buried in London.

John Knill was an extraordinary character and a man of considerable ability. A lawyer and a Customs Official, he was a patron of the arts, a collector, a treasure hunter and a dabbler in politics. He was also responsible for the building of Smeaton's Pier in St Ives harbour, and was sent by the British government to Jamaica, where he devised a plan to prevent the smuggling of coffee. The planters of the island treated him with such lavish hospitality that he was able to bank £1,500 on his return, and there was speculation as to the source of his wealth. The erection of the steeple caused raised eyebrows: was it a day-marker to help the smugglers whom Knill was ostensibly trying to catch? Who knows?

As well as erecting the steeple, Knill established a charity to benefit St Ives and ensure his life was remembered. He dictated that once every five years, a portion of his gift should be distributed between the Mayor of St Ives for a dinner for himself and Knill's trustees. The rest was to be given to ten maidens – the daughters of seamen, fishermen or tinners; two of their widows; the family with the largest number of legitimate children under the age of ten, and one musician. These people had then to proceed to the memorial and perform a ceremony of remembrance.

The money ran out long ago, but the ceremony is still performed every five years. The chosen persons and the civic dignitaries process to the memorial, following the fiddler who leads them playing the tune of the Furry Dance. Once there, the children dance, a hymn is sung and Knill is remembered as he intended.

Paper 'pasties' with hake and onions

The people of St Ives are referred to locally as 'St Ives hakes', and hake with onions is a very traditional Cornish treat whenever this delicious fish is available. Purists will recognize this recipe as slightly different from the traditional Cornish way of cooking hake and onions, which is similar in method but substitutes milk for the cider and serves the whole thing with mashed potatoes. Well seasoned, it's a delicious and soothing supper dish, which I like to serve with new potatoes and a green vegetable. I used tarragon here, but fennel, dill or just parsley would be fine.

Sauté the onions gently in three-quarters of the butter until a light gold colour, then add the cider and simmer until almost all of the liquid is evaporated. Set aside.

Preheat the oven to 200°C.

Prepare your paper cases by cutting four heart shapes out of baking parchment – as big as you can make them within the standard width of the parchment. Divide the onion mixture into four and place on one side of each parchment heart. Top with the fish and the herbs and season. Fold over the parchment, matching up the edges, and start to fold and crimp the edge just as if you were making a Cornish pasty. Make sure the parcels are tightly sealed and put on to a baking tray. Melt the rest of the butter and brush the paper cases.

Lay your parcels on a baking tray and bake for 7–8 minutes in the hot oven. The paper should brown nicely. Take each parcel to the table on its own plate so that your diners get the benefit of the lovely smells as they open their paper 'pasties'.

Paper 'pasty' with hake and onions

St Endellion Music Festival

St. Endellion! St. Endellion! The name is like a ring of bells.

> *Collins Guide to the Parish Churches of England and Wales*, ed. John Betjeman

The late Poet Laureate, Sir John Betjeman (1906–84), said the four corners of St Endellion's tower peep at you like a hare in a cornfield, popping over the brow of the hill as you approach. When you get to it, St Endellion is the most feminine of churches. It has wonderfully carved wooden pew ends, a delicate frieze and a beautiful ceiling. However, the loveliest thing to be seen there is the saint herself, depicted in a gorgeous modern icon holding a single barley straw in blessing.

We know about St Endellion from the work of Nicholas Roscarrock, a Catholic recusant of the sixteenth century who wrote a book on the lives of the saints. Roscarrock was born at a farm in St Endellion's parish, and no doubt this saintly dairymaid held a special significance for him.

Roscarrock says that St Endellion was one of the children of the Welsh King Brychan, and that she was born about AD 470. Her claim to fame as a saint is that she restored to life the man who killed her cow – and the cow as well. When she was dying she directed her followers to place her body on a sled to be pulled by two unguided bullocks, and where they halted so would she. They pulled her to the top of a hill, and the church was built on their resting place.

There could be no more delightful setting for a music festival, and one is held here twice yearly. The St Endellion Music Festival is now over 50 years old, making it more established than many of the 'traditional' but actually 'resurrected' festivals.

The special atmosphere of St Endellion's church has made both it and the festival a magnet and a refuge for musicians from all over the world. What began as a few friends coming down to restore the ancient rectory and put on a few *ad hoc* concerts has become a significant date in the musical calendar. There are exciting plans to turn the buildings around the church into a centre for music and spirituality. Betjeman, who loved the church and is buried at nearby St Enodoc, would surely have approved.

Spiced cherries

St Endellion is also the name of a delicious, soft, brie-like cheese, made at Trevarrian near Newquay. Naming a cheese for this saint is appropriate, as she reputedly lived on milk.

I don't want to mess about with something as lovely as St Endellion cheese, but it would be nice to have something both beautiful and delicious with it.

These preserves should be kept in a cool, dark place, and eaten within a couple of months since the cherries do shrivel if you keep them longer than that.

For the spicing, you could also use star anise, allspice or cloves, but don't overdo it.

Make the syrup by heating the vinegar and sugar in a stainless steel pan. Bring it slowly to the boil, and then add the salt and spices and simmer for 10 minutes. Leave until completely cold – preferably overnight. Sterilize the preserving jars. I usually put them through my dishwasher to sterilize, and use them just after they come out and have dried off.

Wash and dry the cherries, leaving the stalks on and discarding any blemished ones. Pack the cherries into the sterilized jars, adding thyme and bay to each one. Top up with the syrup and seal. You might have some syrup left – it depends on the size of your jars. Leave for a week before eating with the delicious cheese.

Keep in a cool dark place and eat within a couple of months.

Spiced cherries

Goldsithney Charter Fair... August

Goldsithney Charter Fair takes place in early August. In his classic *Popular Romances of the West of England* (1865), Robert Hunt says:

> On the 5th of August, St James's day, a fayre is held here, which was originally held in the Church-town of Sithney near Helston. In olden time, the good St Perran the Little gave to the wrestlers in his parish a glove as the prize, and the winner of the glove was permitted to collect the market toll on the day of the feast, and to appropriate the money to his own use. The winner of the glove lived in the Church-town of Sithney, and for long years the right of holding the fair remained undisputed. At length the miners of Goldsithney resolved to contest the prize, and they won it, since which time the fair has been held in that village, they paying to the poor of the parish of Sithney one shilling as compensation.

The origins of the fair at Goldsithney are lost in time. The Domesday Book refers to the village as 'Plen-Goyl-Sithney', the 'Field of the Fair of Sithney', certainly dating the fair to pre-Norman times. Fair Days were not just an opportunity for fun and meeting with friends and family. They were also when rents and other dues were paid. For Goldsithney, the fair was also the day of a Leat Court when the Lord of the Manor ensured that all the obligations he could demand from the villagers had been carried out, and any transgressors were fined.

One of the primary activities at Goldsithney Fair is Cornish wrestling, in which the combatants wear jackets and attempt to throw each other by grabbing their opponent's coat. It has been a sport in the west of England since earliest times, with the first written record coming from Richard Carew in *The Survey of Cornwall* (1602):

> Wrastling is as full of manliness, more delightful and less dangerous [than hurling] ... for you shall hardly find an assembly of boys in Devon and Cornwall, where the most untowardly amongst them will not as readily give you a muster of this exercise as you are prone to require it.

Cornish fairings

You can picture the scene at the Fair – the local lads eager to show off their wrestling prowess, the lasses keen to watch. Maybe, when the match was over, a pretty girl might expect a few fairings as a token of affection.

Goldsithney Charter Fair is one of those real community events organized by the village for the village. There's music and singing, a dog show, stalls selling lots of lovely things to eat, lots of drinking and lots of fun.

Fairings – originally edible treats sold at fairs, later in Cornwall ginger biscuits – are sold all over Cornwall, and are a favourite for visitors to take home. Some old recipes use candied peel instead of ginger, which gives a nice citrus hit. They are really easy to make. If you have any left over (unlikely), chunk them into softened vanilla ice cream then refreeze. Completely decadent with clotted cream!

Sieve the dry ingredients together, rub in the butter until the mixture is the colour and consistency of sand (a quick blitz in a food processor does it in seconds). Stir in the sugar and ginger. Warm the syrup, pour into the mixture, and mix thoroughly to a stiffish paste.

Preheat the oven to 200°C.

Roll the mixture into walnut-sized balls in the palms of your hands – if you are looking for consistency, each one weighs about 12 g. Place the balls on a greased baking sheet, allowing them room to spread out. Bake for about 10 minutes, moving the baking sheet from the top of the oven to the bottom about half way through baking, or as soon as the biscuits start to brown. The crackled top is how they are supposed to look!

Cornish fairings

Tea Treats and Sunday School Outings

It's easy to forget that centuries ago, most children worked from a very young age. In Cornwall, this often meant doing the ancillary jobs associated with mining, or in areas where there was little mining, children worked long hours in the fields. The Methodist chapel Sunday school was often the only place were these children might be taught to read and write.

The tradition of an annual 'treat' being laid on for the Sunday school scholars started in the early nineteenth century. Children were marched to a hilltop to sing hymns and had to listen to a sermon, after which they would be rewarded with tea and cake.

The treats were often held at Whitsuntide or on the same day as the local fair, in order to tempt the children and their parents away from more worldly pleasures. For the same reason, many tea treats were held during the miners' midsummer holidays, when Victorian ministers believed that idle hands might fall into bad ways.

Tea treats became the cause of much rivalry as to which chapel could provide the most spectacular treat with the biggest band, the most beautiful banners, the largest number of children, and the best tea! By the 1860s, some Sunday school tea treats attracted hundreds of participants. They were hugely enjoyable social occasions, with everyone parading in their best clothes and looking forward to a spectacular feast.

The treat was paid for by the Sunday school scholars themselves. Those with a good attendance record were rewarded with a free or reduced-price ticket. This meant the chapel actually made a profit from the excursion, which was then put towards running the Sunday school for the rest of the year. The tea treat became the public face of a very strong Methodist community, particularly in mining areas. Indeed, the treats were an important way of drawing non-believers into the Methodist fold.

The normal fare at a tea treat was a great spread of saffron buns. These were often called 'revel buns' and, on this occasion only, were made 'as large as cow pats'! Cornish splits with jam and cream were usually on the table, together with slab (fruit) cake and tea. The tea was sweetened as a special treat, Methodists not generally holding with sugar because of its associations with the slave trade.

Cornish cream tea

You will need:

- 500 g plain flour
- ½ tsp fine Cornish sea salt
- 25 g caster sugar
- ½ sachet easy-blend yeast
- 60 g butter
- 250 ml full-fat milk
- Cornish clotted cream, to serve
- strawberry jam or black treacle, to serve

This makes 8 splits.

These days, scones are the norm for a cream tea, but traditionally the vehicle for clotted cream and jam was a Cornish split – a kind of roll made from milk dough. Here's the recipe.

Sift the flour and salt into a bowl and add the sugar and yeast. Melt the butter and warm the milk until tepid, mix together and then add to the flour. Flour varies as to its absorbency, so you may need a little more milk. Knead the dough on a floured board for 10 minutes until really smooth, then leave in a warm place until doubled in size – it takes about 90 minutes.

Knead again briefly and divide into eight balls, then knead and mould each ball until it is perfectly smooth. Place on a lined baking sheet and leave to rise again for about 45 minutes.

Preheat the oven to 180°C.

Put the baking sheet into the oven and bake for 20 minutes. You may want to cover the splits with a loose sheet of foil or paper about halfway through – they should be a delicate pale gold, not brown.

Leave to cool, then split the rolls and slather with clotted cream and jam – or for an even more special treat, with a spoonful of black treacle instead of jam. The Cornish call this 'thunder and lightning'.

A Cornish cream tea

Newlyn Fish Festival...
August Bank Holiday

The village of Newlyn, clinging snugly to the east-facing slope of Mount's Bay, is an extraordinary place – an important fishing centre, one of the first communities to resist redevelopment, and a famous nineteenth-century artists' colony.

Newlyn is a lively fishing port. The harbour fills with fishing boats large and small, and there is a fish market most mornings. Because of its easy reach to the Western Approaches, over 50 species of edible fish are landed at Newlyn. Much of the catch is shipped up country and to Spain and France. Breton lorries take their loads of seafood to be eaten by visitors to Brittany who little suspect that their *fruits de mer* are actually fruits of Cornwall. The village is home to fish-processing, ice-making, chandleries and several really good fish shops. There are also some great pubs serving thirsty fishermen.

Pilchards were the lifeblood of Newlyn, but mackerel and herring were almost as important. Over £80,000 worth of mackerel was landed in 1905 – a vast amount for those days. The hardships of Newlyners' lives in the nineteenth century are graphically captured in the paintings of Stanhope Forbes (1857–1947) and his followers, who settled in Newlyn in the 1880s. Forbes' first painting of the town, *A Fish Sale on a Cornish Beach*, was exhibited at the Royal Academy in 1885 and led to hundreds more paintings by him, his pupils and the other artists who formed the colony. The Penlee Gallery in Penzance houses many important examples of their work.

It was Len Scott, then head of the Newlyn Fishermen's Mission, who started the Newlyn Fish Festival in 1991. The festival's aims are to allow 'the fishermen of Newlyn the opportunity to show their industry off to the wider public who, perhaps, know little about commercial fishing or its problems'. The festival was a huge success from the outset. Thousands of people flock to Newlyn to look at the boats, the stalls of every sort, and to watch filleting competitions and cookery demonstrations, see extraordinary displays of fish and eat delicious fishy dishes.

Marinated mackerel

This delicious fishy dish is an adaptation from *Cornish Recipes Ancient and Modern*, collected by Edith Martin and first published by the Cornish Federation of Women's Institutes in 1929.

I buy my mackerel from the mackerel man who sits daily with his fish in a giant cool box in a little van on a lay-by just outside Penzance. When I asked him how he cooked marinated mackerel, he said the same way as his mother, with lemon peel and ginger. The flavourings of this dish are almost infinitely variable. Try adding parsley, tarragon or even garlic with lime, ginger and chilli – whatever you fancy, just stick to the vinegar part of the method.

Ask your fishmonger to scale and gut the fish, take the heads off, flatten them out and remove their backbones.

Preheat the oven to 160°C.

Lay the fish flat, skin-side down, in a flat-bottomed dish. Sprinkle with the onion and the other seasoning ingredients, then just cover with vinegar. Put into the oven and bake gently for an hour. Cool slightly, then remove the individual fish to a serving dish, and strain the liquid over. Refrigerate and serve cold. Decorate with parsley, if you wish. The cooked marinated fish will have developed a wonderful meaty texture.

Marinated mackerel

The Cornish Gorsedd

In *Geographica*, his huge text on the geography of the known world, the Greek writer Strabo (63 BC–AD 24) referred to the Celtic tradition of honouring the bards – the singers and poets who preserved the history and traditions of the tribes living on the western fringes of Europe. Local tribal chiefs would have a bard on hand to entertain the company after supper with songs and stories from a long oral tradition now completely lost.

We know from ancient Welsh sources that there were three major locations where the bards periodically came together for the purpose of ceremony and competitions in music, poetry and literature. One of these 'Gorsedd' places was Beisgawen, now widely accepted as being Boscawen-Un, the ancient stone circle also called the Nine Maidens, near St Buryan in West Penwith.

Modern interest in these old keepers of the culture began in the late eighteenth century with one famously eccentric Welshman, called Iolo Morganwg, who researched what little was known about the ancient bards and then made up the rest! Just as the last few native Cornish speakers were dying out, Morganwg established the Welsh Gorsedd, and that led in the late nineteenth century to interest among scholars in similarly restoring the bardic tradition in Cornwall, partly as a means to save and revive the Cornish language.

It was only right then that in 1928 the first meeting of the newly formed Gorsedd of Cornwall (*Gorsedh Kernow* in Cornish) was held at Boscawen-Un stone circle. With the support of bards from Wales, a Cornish Grand Bard was ceremoniously installed and the Cornish Gorsedd was instituted.

The Cornish bards now come together annually for the same purposes as their ancient predecessors. *Gorsedh Kernow* promotes the Celtic spirit of Cornwall and the Cornish language. It is regarded as a great honour to wear the druidical dress of the Gorsedd, and those invited to do so choose a bardic name which describes them, such as 'John from the North' or 'Sea Maiden', a tradition which goes back to the bards of medieval Wales.

Every year the Cornish bards meet at their chosen Gorsedd place and process with dignified ceremony. The venue is moved around the county to ensure everyone gets the chance to observe these revered custodians of Cornish culture. Members of the Cornish diaspora come from all over the world to join them – many of them are bards themselves, and are often descendants of brave Cornish miners who sought their fortunes in newer worlds.

It's all very solemn, and a far cry from the Gorsedd meetings of ancient times which probably involved a great deal of feasting and heavy drinking. There are now numerous competitions held in association with the Cornish Gorsedd, for poems and other creative endeavours… and finally, after all that culture, there is a jolly good tea for the bards, and a Gorsedd concert for the local community.

Cornish under-roast

Here is that most hearty of Cornish suppers – an under-roast, just the thing for Gorsedd eve to set up a Bard for all that processing.

The cooking in most Cornish kitchens used to be done on a cast iron Cornish range, which dictated the way that things were cooked – usually with the greatest economy of fuel.

A Cornish under-roast can be made with any sort of meat, but cheap cuts such as beef shin that benefit from long, slow cooking are best. About 150 g per head is a generous helping, but quantities are hard to give, so this is a method rather than a recipe. I like this with a leafy green vegetable, especially buttered cabbage, and mustard or horse-radish sauce on the side.

Preheat the oven to 160°C.

Peel and halve about one large roasting potato per person. Boil them in salted water for five minutes, then slice them and put half the sliced potatoes in the bottom of a roasting tin. Season well. Lay the meat on top and then cover with the rest of the potatoe slices. Season again and dribble some vegetable oil over. Add the stock, or water will do. Cover the dish with foil, and put into the oven for an hour. Take off the foil and cook for another hour. All the water will have been absorbed; the potatoes should be crisp and brown on top but melting underneath, and the meat cooked to tenderness.

Cornish under-roast

Michaelmas... 29 September

Together with St Piran and St Petroc, the Archangel St Michael is one of the patron saints of Cornwall. In Celtic regions, he is often associated with hilltops, and St Michael's Mount has been a holy place probably since there have been holy places.

'The Mount', as it is referred to locally, has had a number of names. In classical times it was very likely the island known as Ictis, the legendary source of tin from the west. In the Cornish language it is known as 'Karrek Loos y'n Koos', meaning the 'grey rock in the woods', an indication of the changes of sea level that the coast of Cornwall has witnessed over the millennia.

We know for a fact that for centuries the Mount was an important market on an ancient trading route. Archaeological evidence shows that tin was being traded there as long ago as 350 BC. The market was a source of products from all over the known world: oils, silks and spices came from the Mediterranean; tin and precious metals, furs, wool and hunting dogs went the other way. This market may even be the original source of the beautifully scented narcissus flowers native to the Mediterranean area and now regarded as indigenous on the offshore islands of Cornwall.

St Michael's Mount market features in the legend of Tristan and Iseult, which was written about 1170. The author, Béroul, describes how the hermit Ogrin visits St Michael's Mount to buy fine wool, silks and linen cloth for Iseult, so that she might be suitably clad for her betrothed husband, King Mark.

The Benedictines erected a monastery on the Mount, which was consecrated in 1144. It became a major pilgrimage destination, and a significant stopping point on the network of pilgrim routes across Europe, in particular for those making their way to Santiago de Compostela from Wales and Ireland. The route from St Ives to St Michael's Mount is now a designated footpath, way-marked with the symbolic pilgrims' scallop shell.

On the top of the Mount is a precipitous stone chair; to sit on it you have to hang your legs over the steep drop. When a marriage takes place on the island, the newly weds are supposed to race to the chair, and it is said that the first to sit in it will have dominion over the other for the duration of the marriage! It's a very stiff climb, so perhaps the victor deserves the prize.

On St Michael's Day – Michaelmas – legend says that St Michael's celestial fight with the devil caused Satan to fall to earth on a bramble bush, making the eating of blackberries after 29 September inadvisable because the Devil has cursed and spat on them – or worse.

Extra rich bramble and apple pie

To counteract all the devilish activity of St Michael's Day, the Michaelmas recipe has to be that culinary marriage made in heaven – bramble and apple pie – traditionally made in an enamel pie dish. But make sure you pick the blackberries before that day!

Preheat the oven to 180°C.

Divide the pastry into two portions, one slightly larger than the other. Roll out and line an enamel pie dish with the smaller portion. Lay the apple slices on the pastry and sprinkle over half the sugar. Put the blackberries on top of the apple, sprinkle with the cornflour, and add the rest of the sugar, reserving a teaspoonful of sugar to sprinkle on the lid.

Top with the pastry lid, crimp the edge lightly, and make two little cuts in the top for the steam. Decorate with little pastry leaves if you have some off-cuts. Brush the pastry with the egg or the cream; sprinkle with any remaining sugar, and put the pie on to a baking tray. Bake for 35–40 minutes. Keep an eye on it and cover with foil if it is getting too brown.

Now do my Grandma's trick. Take the pie out of the oven and let it cool just a little. Very gently put a sharp, thin, wide-bladed knife or a spatula under the pie lid and ease it off all the way around, but don't remove it. Raise the lid at one side and sneak a knob of butter on top of the hot fruit. Let the lid down again. Serve with cream.

Extra rich bramble and apple pie

Harvest Time: Crying the Neck

In Cornwall years ago, the last sheaf cut at harvest time was called 'the neck', and in common with many other country districts when it was cut, the end of the harvest was celebrated by the ceremony of 'Crying the Neck'. In *Cornish Feasts and Folk Lore*, Miss Courtney tells us that the oldest reaper called out, 'I hav'et! I hav'et! I hav'et', and his companions replied, 'What hav'ee? What hav'ee? What hav'ee?' He then shouted, 'A Neck! A Neck! A Neck!' and they all replied, 'Hurrah!'

After the harvest comes the Harvest Supper, sometimes called the Mell Supper, the word 'mell' coming from the Old Norse word *mele*, meaning grain. This was an occasion for general rejoicing, and the harvest workers feasted on pasties, cold meats, junket and saffron cake, often washed down with a temperance beverage – herby beer made from Mason's Extract of Herbs ('a six-penny bottle makes eight gallons'). For those who hadn't signed the pledge of teetotalism, cider was the standard drink.

Until the 1840s, harvest celebrations were purely secular and almost pagan. Then enter on to the scene the Reverend Robert Stephen Hawker (1803–75). When Hawker became vicar of Morwenstow in 1834, the Church of England had neglected it for years – as it had much of Cornwall. The Methodist tradition in the South West is a legacy of that. Morwenstow really was a Wild West area, but it suited the young cleric and he ministered to all – sailors, fishermen, smugglers, wreckers and miners.

Hawker was a real eccentric. He married twice, once dressed up as a mermaid; excommunicated his cat for mousing on Sundays, and habitually wore a claret-coloured coat, blue fisherman's jersey, long sea-boots, a pink hat and a shawl made from a yellow horse blanket. He talked to the birds, invited his nine cats into church, and kept a pet pig.

On 13 September 1843, Hawker put up a notice in the church for a new kind of service:

Let us gather together in the chancel of our church, and there receive, in the bread of the new corn, that Blessed Sacrament which was ordained to strengthen and refresh our souls.

Harvest Festival was born.

Hawker built a tiny hut on the cliffs near his home, using timbers from the wreckage of the *Alonzo*. The hut is still there; it belongs to the National Trust. He used it to commune with nature, write poetry and smoke a little opium. So my harvest offering for the Reverend Hawker is a sweet loaf stuffed with the seeds of *Papaver somniferum* – the opium poppy.

*Poppy
seed roll*

Poppy seed roll

You will need

For the sweet dough:

- 250 ml milk, full-fat or semi-skimmed
- 140 g melted butter
- 2 eggs
- ½ tsp vanilla extract,
- 500 g strong plain flour
- 1½ tsp fine Cornish sea salt
- 60 g sugar
- 2 tsp easy-blend yeast

For the filling:

- 120 g sugar
- 100 ml milk
- 120 g poppy seeds, plus extra for sprinkling
- 80 g sultanas, chopped
- 2 tbsp honey
- 1 tbsp candied peel
- grated rind of a lemon
- 1 egg, separated

For the glacé icing:

- 3 heaped tbsp icing sugar
- 1 dessert spn hot water

This serves 8–10.

Sweet dough: Mix all ingredients in a large bowl. Turn on to a floured surface and knead until the dough is smooth and elastic. Put back in the bowl, cover with a cloth, and let it rise in a warm place until doubled in size – about an hour.

Filling: Put sugar and milk in a pan, bring to the boil and simmer for 5 minutes. Add remaining ingredients. Bring to the boil again and simmer for 5 more minutes; it will be quite thick and will thicken more as it cools. Beat the egg white, and when the filling is cool, fold it in.

Turn the risen, puffy dough on to the floured surface and roll into a rectangle about 2 cm thick. Spread on the filling.

Roll the dough into a sausage with the seam underneath, tuck the ends under and place on a greased baking tray. Allow to rise for 30 minutes. Beat the egg yolk and brush it over the dough twice to make it rich and shiny.

Preheat the oven to 190°C. Bake for about 35 minutes, until golden. If it gets very brown cover lightly with foil. Let it cool, dribble over icing, and sprinkle with poppy seeds if you wish.

Callington Honey Fair… October

Callington in east Cornwall calls itself 'the town below the hill', the hill in question being Kit Hill, which is a 'Marilyn', meaning that its summit is more than 150 metres above the lowest slope. Kit Hill (the name derives from kite, the bird) was given to the people of Cornwall in 1985 by Prince Charles as Duke of Cornwall to mark the birth of his first son, Prince William, the heir to the Duchy; it is now a country park.

Kit Hill is the highest spot in the Tamar Valley Area of Outstanding Natural Beauty. From the top you can see the Eddystone Lighthouse, around Plymouth Sound and over to Bude on the north coast. The hill has been used by humans for over 5,000 years, from prehistoric times through the long years of mineral exploitation and right up to the present day when it sits quietly in the sunshine like an old miner after a lifetime of hard work.

Callington too has a long history, and is one of the main contenders for the site of 'Celliwig', the ancient capital of Cornwall and site of the court of King Arthur. In 1267, King Henry III granted the town a charter to hold a market, and one has been held there con-tinuously since that time. From the early nineteenth century, a Honey Fair was held every August and this continued until the Second World War. In 1978, the tradition was re-established, and Callington Honey Fair is now one of the largest street fairs in Cornwall.

It is still a place for the county's beekeepers to meet at the end of summer and compare their experiences of the season. There are competitions for the best honey, honey products such as combs and beeswax, and for recipes made with honey. I love the fact the competition details and rules are given in a document known as 'The Honey Schedule'.

Many very old Cornish recipe books contain recipes for 'sweet wine' – the old Cornish term for mead or metheglyn, mead's spiced variant. Both are made by fermenting honey into alcohol, and it's safe to assume that bee-keeping has a long history in the county. Indeed, the First and Last Inn near Land's End used to boast that the monks who apparently ran a pilgrims' rest house on the site gave local newly weds enough mead to last them for one phase of the moon – giving rise to the term 'honeymoon'. Well, maybe.

Like apiarists all over the world, Cornish beekeepers have their own superstitions, and a nineteenth-century account of beekeeping on Trencrom Hill, near St Ives, records the hives being covered with black cloths when there was a death in the house of their keeper. My beekeeping acquaintances say it's important to tell the bees any household news, or else they may feel neglected and move on to a friendlier home.

Metheglyn tart

You will need:

- shortcrust pastry made with 220 g plain flour and 120 g butter, or 375 g ready-made pastry
- 120 g stewed cooking apples, cooled and sweetened with 2 tbsp white sugar and ½ tsp vanilla extract
- 1 tbsp golden syrup
- 6 tbsp good local honey
- juice and zest of half a lemon
- 1 tsp ground ginger
- ½ tsp cinnamon
- ¼ tsp nutmeg
- 120 g fresh white breadcrumbs
- about 1 tbsp icing sugar, to decorate
- Cornish clotted cream or rich vanilla ice cream, to serve

This serves 6.

net and transferred the design to a small card. Then I cut out the bee shape very carefully. I held the card over the tart and sifted about a tablespoon of icing sugar over the card using my coffee strainer. Very cunning!

Preheat the oven to 180°C.

Line a shallow, 25-cm plate or flan dish with pastry. Spread the apple over the pastry.

Warm the syrup and the honey in a pan and add the lemon juice. Stir in the remaining ingredients. Pour over the apple and bake for 30 minutes, or until golden.

Decorate the tart with sifted icing sugar.

Serve warm with clotted cream or rich vanilla ice cream.

This recipe for honey tart is a variation of one in the late Lady St Levan's book, *A Cornish Choice of Recipes* (1991). I've tinkered with it a bit and added more spice to make it reminiscent of the spicy taste of metheglyn.

To make the busy bees on the top, I downloaded a free stencil of a bee from the inter-

Metheglyn tart

The Nelson Thanksgiving Service at Madron… October

Every year on the nearest Sunday to 21 October, there is a very special service in the parish church of St Maddern near Penzance. It commemorates the victory of the British Fleet at the Battle of Trafalgar in 1805, and the death of Admiral Lord Nelson. Civic dignitaries process to the church and the Trafalgar Banner is unfurled. These days they parade a replica of the original, now very fragile banner, which is permanently displayed in Penlee House, Penzance.

The story goes that after the decisive sea battle was won, the British schooner HMS *Pickle* sailed with all speed towards Falmouth carrying the despatches with details of the outcome, including the death of Britain's hero, Admiral Lord Nelson. On their way they encountered a local fishing boat and passed on the news of the battle and of Nelson's death to its crew. When the fishermen arrived back in Mount's Bay, they made straight for the Assembly Rooms in Chapel Street, Penzance and announced the news to the Mayor and the assembled company at the ball being held there. Mayor Thomas Giddy led his townsfolk immediately up to Madron church – the mother church of Penzance – to mourn and to celebrate. A simple banner was hastily prepared for the occasion.

A service of commemoration for the Battle of Trafalgar was first held in 1946, when there was also much to give thanks for. There has been a service every year since then.

Back in 1805, some residents of Cornwall would have greeted with mixed feelings the end of 25 years of on-off warfare. Throughout the county, several hundred French prisoners of war were living on parole in locals' homes. Some had been in Cornwall for years, allowed to live freely as long as the authorities knew where they were. Many of these French sailors made a living by fashioning trinkets, plastering ceilings, teaching dancing, drawing and languages. Many had married local girls, and surnames such as Rouffignac, Gascoigne and Paulet began to appear in the records as a generation of French-Cornish babies were born.

Mourn for the Brave

the immortal NELSON'S gone

His last Sea fight is fought

his work of Glory done.

Hedgerow relish

You will need:

- 1.5 kg mixed hedgerow fruit (blackberries, sloes and elderberries), leaves and stalks removed, washed and picked over for insects
- 500 g tart apples – windfalls are fine, peeled and chopped
- 375 g chopped onions
- 500 ml white wine vinegar
- 1 tsp ground allspice
- 1 tsp ground cinnamon
- 4 cloves
- 6 black peppercorns
- generous pinch chilli powder
- 2 tbsp Cornish sea salt
- 500 g sugar
- 6 or 7 x 500-g jars

This makes about 3 kg relish.

The parish of Madron is a wonderful place for foraging. Up the old miners' tracks are blackberries, elderberries and sloes in abundance. You might also find an ancient gnarled apple tree with some delicious little fruit. To preserve autumn in a jar, I make this fruity ketchup to serve with cold meats, cheese and sausages or pork pie throughout the winter. The proportions of fruit don't matter very much. Leave for a couple of weeks before using. This keeps very well.

Put everything except the sugar into a heavy-bottomed pan and slowly bring up to the boil. Simmer gently until it is all soft and mushy, about 20–25 minutes.

I like to cool the mixture at this point, because the next stage is easier (and safer) if it's not boiling hot. Rub the pulp though a nylon sieve with the back of a wooden spoon. This is quite hard work, but the smooth result is really worth it.

Rinse out the pan and return the pulp to the stove, reheat and add the sugar, stirring over medium heat until it has all dissolved. Now boil briskly for 20 minutes until thick. Keep checking it's not sticking to the pan – you don't want to burn it. Pour into warm, sterilized jars. I usually put them through my dishwasher to sterilize, and use them just after they have dried off and come out.

Hedgerow relish

Allantide – *Nos Calan Gwaf…*
October

The three days from 31 October to 2 November are associated in both pagan and Christian mythologies with the remembrance of the dead and the spirit world they supposedly inhabit. In the far west of Cornwall, the nearest Saturday to Halloween was celebrated as Allantide, or sometimes Hallantide. Miss Courtney, in her *Cornish Feasts and Folk Lore*, describes it thus:

The shops in Penzance would display Allan apples, which were highly polished large apples. On the day itself, these apples were given as gifts to each member of the family as a token of good luck. Older girls would place these apples under their pillows and hope to dream of the person whom they would one day marry. A local game is also recorded where two pieces of wood were nailed together in the shape of a cross. It was then suspended with four candles on each outcrop of the cross shape. Allan apples would then be suspended under the cross. The goal of the game was to catch the apples in your mouth, with hot wax being the penalty for slowness or inaccuracy.

There was a special market at the end of October to sell Allan apples, and Penzance Farmers' Market now celebrates this tradition as part of the nationwide Apple Day celebrations.

Allantide was when the membrane between the physical and the spirit world was supposedly stretched thin enough to permit communication, so it was a traditional time for fortune-telling. The most bizarre practice was to use your left leg garter to tie the front door key between the pages of a Bible at the Song of Solomon. When the key was removed, it was said to twirl around when your true sweetheart's name was mentioned!

I wonder whether these Cornish traditions are left over from pre-Christian times when, as the pastoral year came to an end, there was a festival to mark this turning point. The old Gaelic word for the festival is *Samain*, suggesting 'summer's end', and at this time of year there are long established Celtic traditions of dressing up as malevolent spirits.

So there is definitely a numinous undertone of darkness at this time of year. The barns may be full, but the dark months are ahead. To the Anglo Saxons, November was *blod-monath*, or 'blood month' – the traditional month for the slaughter of animals. Leaves are falling – death is literally in the air.

Penzance apple cake

You will need:

- 220 g plain flour
- 120 g butter
- 220 g currants
- 1 tsp ground ginger
- 60 g mixed peel
- 1 tsp cinnamon
- 1 tsp bicarbonate of soda
- 5 tbsp full-fat milk
- 2 eggs, beaten
- 2 dessert apples, peeled and very thinly sliced
- 20 g dark brown sugar, to decorate
- 20-cm cake tin

This serves 8–10.

For Allantide, I've made a Penzance cake from an old local recipe and put a layer of apples in the middle. When you peel the apples, throw the peel over your shoulder and it will form the initial of the man you will marry. Don't do this if you are already married – it may form the wrong letter! Served in hefty wedges, this is a great cake for a late picnic. Try it with a slice of Cornish Yarg cheese.

Preheat the oven to 150°C.

Grease a 20-cm cake tin thoroughly. Rub the flour and butter together until they resemble breadcrumbs, then put into a mixing bowl and add the rest of the dry ingredients. Beat the eggs and add them to the mixture. Mix the milk with the bicarbonate of soda and stir this into the mixture, adding a little more milk if necessary – you want a mixture that drops softly off your spoon.

Put half the mixture into the tin and lay on the sliced apple, then add the rest of the mixture. Bake at 150°C for about an hour and a half, until golden on top and cooked through.

There is no sugar in this mixture, the sweetness comes from the dried fruit and the apple, but you can sprinkle sugar on top of the cake before baking. Just check it does not scorch.

Penzance apple cake

St Just Feast... November

St Just Feast, held during the week of All Souls' Day in early November, was one of the largest parish celebrations in Cornwall. Almost every village in the country used to have an annual feast day to celebrate the parish saint, but over the centuries most have been discontinued. St Just-in-Penwith has always been a proud and individual town, and its feast was famous. The whole parish gathered together for several days of celebrations in church and chapel, but mostly out in the town square and in the pubs that surround it. 'Santusters' – natives of the town who lived up country – tried to come home for the feast. People flocked into town on foot or by any kind of conveyance possible – the gaily-decked Penzance post chaise, the humble Sennen sand-cart. Nowadays, the Western Hunt holds its opening meet on Feast Monday, with stirrup cups for all in Market Square.

St Just was a mining town, and life was hard. During Feast Week – even more than at Christmas – working people let their hair down. Feasten Monday was a general holiday: mines were silent, only the engine men were still on duty to tend the pumping gear.

There were games and revels, wrestling, pitch and toss and Punch and Judy. Girls put on their new hats, boys showed off their skills in the shooting galleries. Old men exchanged tales in the pubs, which swarmed with visitors from mining communities world-wide.

Fiddlers played in the pubs, and local choirs entertained the crowds. When the beer and toddy flowed, the voices of the drinkers swelled out across the square.

People celebrated at home too, and the hospitality was legendary. Women cooked for days to prepare for visitors and home-comers. One of the most popular dishes was what the French would call a *pot au feu* – a huge cauldron simmering over the open fire containing a savoury joint of beef, a fowl a piece of bacon and lots of vegetables. There would be steamed apples – it was Allantide too – and there were the legendary Cornish pies and pasties of rabbit, pilchard or squab.

After supper there would be plenty of 'custom' (smuggled spirits). St Just was a smugglers' haven, and the Santusters were only used to good French brandy and the best Holland gin.

Pigeon pie

Cornish Recipes Ancient and Modern has seven recipes for squab (pigeon) pie, the game meat of the poor. Where squab was unobtainable, the pie was made with mutton. Some recipes, like mine, use both.

A traditional Moroccan dish, P'astilla, is also a pigeon pie. The seasonings and filling are exactly the same as in the Cornish version. So might Cornish squab pie be evidence of an ancient link between Cornwall and the Barbary Coast (as saffron might be), or was it a leftover from medieval times when much British cooking was flavoured with spices from the east?

I like to serve this pie with a leafy vegetable and extra gravy. Don't be put off by the spice and apple, it's delicious. It is also good cold with pickles or Hedgerow relish (page 102).

Take the breasts off the pigeons, skin, slice thinly and set aside. Put the pigeon carcasses and sliced lamb in a pan and cover with water. Bring to the boil, cover and simmer gently for 40 minutes. Take out the lamb, trim off the fat, cut into small pieces and set aside. Continue to simmer the stock until reduced by a third.

Put the onion and apple into a bowl. Add the cold lamb and raw pigeon breasts, season well, and add the mixed spice and currants.

Preheat the oven to 160°C.

Roll out half the pastry and line a pie dish, pile on the filling, dribble on some of the stock (about 4–5 tbsp), and cover with the rest of the pastry. Seal the pie edges well, decorate with pastry trimmings and brush with beaten egg. Make a small slit in the lid to let the steam escape.

Pigeon pie

Place on a baking tray in the oven and bake for an hour or until the pastry is crisp and golden. Make gravy by thickening and seasoning the pigeon stock.

Montol... 21 December

On the night of the winter solstice, Penzance is thronged with masked revellers, guize dancing and bearing paper lanterns in the Rivers of Fire procession. It's all for Montol – the old Cornish midwinter festival. Guize dancing is the Cornish equivalent of mumming – a celebration of mischief, misrule and topsy-turvy.

Before the lantern procession starts, the Lord of Misrule is chosen from among the revellers by the old custom of drawing a bean from a bag. The Lord leads young and old – all disguised, masked and wearing extraordinary costumes – through the streets where they are joined by Penzance's 'obby 'oss, Penglaz, to the music of the Turkey Rhubarb Band. Eventually, holding their lanterns, everyone congregates around a burning brazier on Lescudjack Hill, the site of an Iron Age fort overlooking the town. Later that night the figure of a man will be chalked on the Yule Mock, or Log, before it is burned and Penzance looks forward to the death of the old year and the birth of the new.

In earlier times, guize dancers might do traditional dances in the streets, or even enter unbidden in peoples' homes! Cornish carols were sung in the streets – a tradition upheld in modern Montol with the Cornish Carol Service.

The word *montol* was first translated from Cornish to English in 1700, and means 'balance' – the point when the year balances between dark and light. Montol also balances with the town's midsummer festival of Golowan (page 56). Today's Montol celebrations are like many festivals of this sort, the revival of a very old tradition, but it's amazing how brief the non-observance of Montol was. It was only discontinued in 1914, and lots is known about it, partly because William Botterell, in his *Traditions and Hearthside Stories of West Cornwall* (1870), described it thus:

During the early part of the last century the costume of the guise dancers often consisted of such antique finery as would now raise envy in the heart of a collector. The chief glory of the men lay in their cocked hats which were surmounted with plumes and decked with streamers and

ribbons. The girls were no less magnifi-
cently attired with steeple crowned hats,
stiff bodied gowns, bag skirts or trains and
ruffles hanging from their elbows.

Spicy parsnip, squash and apple soup with hog's pudding croûtons

You will need:

- 1 kg mixed 'hard' vegetables, peeled and roughly chopped
- 1 large Bramley apple, peeled and roughly chopped
- 2 onions, peeled and finely chopped
- 2 cloves garlic, peeled and finely chopped
- 1.5 l vegetable or chicken stock (a cube is fine)
- 1 tsp cumin seeds
- 1 tsp coriander seeds
- 4 cardamom pods, de-seeded
- pinch dried chilli flakes
- 1 tsp ground turmeric
- 1 tsp ground ginger
- Cornish sea salt and freshly ground black pepper
- vegetable oil
- 120 g hog's pudding, black pudding or a thick slice of good bread, to garnish
- chopped fresh coriander, to garnish (optional)

This serves 6.

It gets chilly, even in Cornwall, in December, so here's a winter warmer to give some internal central heating on a cold night.

Hog's pudding is a dense, white, spicy sausage particular to Cornwall and Devon. For what I call the 'hard vegetables' you could mix parsnips, squash, swedes, carrots or celeriac. This soup uses hog's pudding as a delicious croûton on the top. Black pudding would do as well, although it would be different, as would ordinary croûtons. The star and moon shapes add a festive touch.

Roast the whole spices, then grind with the powdered ones. Cook the onions and the garlic in 2 tbsp oil until translucent, then add the spices, vegetables and apple. Stir together well to coat with the spices, and sweat for a few minutes, taking care the vegetables don't catch. Add the stock, bring to the boil, cover and simmer until all is soft. Then blitz with a stick blender or in a liquidizer, and check the seasoning.

Cut out croûtons with star- or moon-shaped cutters and fry in a little oil. Serve the soup garnished with croûtons and coriander.

Spicy parsnip, squash and apple soup with hog's pudding croûtons

Tom Bawcock's Eve…
23 December

A merry plaas you may believe
Woz Mowsel 'pon Tom Bawcock's Eve.
To be theer then oo wudn wesh
To sup o sibm soorts o fesh!

From *Tom Bawcock's Eve*
by Robert Morton Nance (1873–1959)

The village of Mousehole (pronounced 'mowzull') is about three miles along the coast west of Penzance. It is a stunning collection of tiny cottages clustered on a steep cliff overlooking a picturesque harbour. Most visitors, and there are many, see it during the long, blue tranquil Cornish summer days. But in a winter storm, it can be bleak. For any fishing community, life is perilous, and Mousehole has had more than its share of drama and loss.

On 19 December 1981, the Penlee lifeboat, *Solomon Browne*, with eight men from the village on board, was lost with all hands. The former lifeboat station, and the memorial in nearby Paul church, are moving testimonies to their bravery and sacrifice. Even more moving is the fact that within 24 hours, dozens of men from the village volunteered for the new crew.

In 1595, the village was raided and sacked by the Spaniards. Squire Jenkyn Keigwin was slaughtered outside his home; a plaque on the building – the only one to survive the attack – commemorates his death.

Sometime, long ago, the people of Mousehole were starving because the fishermen had been unable to put to sea during a long period of stormy weather. Tom Bawcock persuaded his crew to sail during a brief lull in the storms, and they came home with a boatful of fish. The village was saved.

To commemorate the occasion, each year on Tom Bawcock's Eve a huge, very special, star gazy pie is made at The Ship Inn for everyone to share. It contains potatoes and fish in a creamy sauce. Peeping through the pastry and gazing at the stars are the heads of the pilchards.

Contributing to the festive air, local children parade through the streets of Mousehole with paper lanterns held high. People come from all over Cornwall to join in the celebration and see the famous Mousehole Christmas lights.

Star gazy pie

You will need:

- 500-g sheet of ready-rolled puff pastry (bought pastry is fine)
- 2 medium potatoes, peeled and cut in small chunks
- 60 g butter
- 60 g flour
- 250 ml fish stock (a cube is fine)
- Cornish sea salt and freshly ground black pepper
- 230 g fresh mixed seafood
- 375 g fish pie mix
- 6 sprats
- 1 egg, beaten, to glaze
- a small, deep pie dish

This serves 4.

As Morton Nance says, star gazy pie contains seven sorts of fish, to feed a large number of people. Here's a domestic version.

First choose your pie dish. I like a small, deepish one, as you get more fish than in a wide, shallow one. You need seven sorts of fish, which is easier than you think. Buy a pack of mixed seafood and a bag of pieces of mixed fish for fish pie. Try to include smoked fish. In this mini-version, you don't want pilchards to dominate, so the stargazers are delicious little sprats. You'll need about six. Depending on the shape of your dish, you may need a pie funnel to hold up the middle.

Par-boil the potatoes for about 5–7 minutes until nearly soft, drain well and set aside. Meanwhile, make the sauce: melt the butter, add the flour and mix to a paste. Add the stock and whisk to eliminate any lumps. Simmer for about 10 minutes until the flour in the sauce is well cooked. Season to taste.

Preheat the oven to 200°C.

Spoon the fish, except for the sprats, and the potatoes into the pie dish and mix together. Pour over the sauce, and season. Place a pie funnel in the middle if needed.

Lift the pastry on to your rolling pin and lay it carefully over the pie dish, covering the fish and sauce. Take a sprat, make a little slit in the pastry near the edge of the pie and insert the fish, tail downwards until its head is just poking through and staring at the sky. Repeat until you have a circle of fish peeping out. Brush the pastry with beaten egg and make sure the edges are well sealed. Bake

Star gazy pie

the pie for about 30 minutes. Cover with foil if it starts to brown too much.

They say that Guinness is the thing with star gazy pie, but I prefer good Cornish cider.

Nadelik Lowen... 25 December

In common with the rest of the country, Cornish homes are traditionally decorated with greenery for the festive season. Bunches of holly and mistletoe that used to be sold on street corners – 'a penn'orth o' Christmas' – were often used to decorate two hoops joined at right angles, perhaps with a lighted candle at the base and apples and oranges tied on for colour. This arrangement would be suspended from a beam in the kitchen until Twelfth Night, serving the same purpose as mistletoe, which is why it was referred to as 'the kissing bush'.

One of the strongest Cornish Christmas traditions was the Yule 'mock' – or 'block' or 'stock' – the Cornish version of the Yule log. A suitable log, often of oak or ash, was debarked and placed on the hearth. It was traditional to chalk or carve a rough figure on to the bare wood to deter witches from entering the house for the next twelve months. As a symbol of prosperity and continuity the block was then lit with a faggot saved from the previous year's log.

Here's a lovely story reported in the *West Briton* in February 1838:

... a certain Mr Lukey... was sitting by the fire when his ears were suddenly assailed by cries resembling those of a child which apparently proceeded from the chimney wherein the stock lay burning... On examining the log he noticed that it contained a little hole, which being too small to admit his fingers he split open with an axe, only to discover to his great astonishment a large toad entombed in the centre!

On Christmas Eve, when the block was burning brightly, everyone stayed up until midnight drinking and singing carols around the hearth. Candles were lit, and sometimes stuck into boxes of sand so the children might dance around them.

Many Cornish towns had their own carol sequences, and even their own words and tunes. The Cornish carol tradition is still strong, and Padstow is the place to hear Cornish carols sung in the streets as they have been for hundreds of years. Few of these carols are written down: they are handed down in families, a treasured part of a vibrant,

living tradition. Padstow has a
carol leader who decides
the route to be followed
by the singers – and what
is to be sung where.
The route varies, but
the carollers sing to the
same houses every year
and there is lots of food
and drink to encourage
them as they process.

One of the carols always
sung in Padstow is 'Harky harky',
based on *Hark the Herald Angels Sing*.
The carollers of Padstow picked it up from
fishermen further west who used Padstow
quay during the winter months. You can
imagine the rivalry between different fishermen – 'Them's the words!' – 'No them's the
words…!'

Yule log

You will need:
- 5 large eggs, separated
- 160 g caster sugar
- 60 g unsweetened cocoa powder
- 200 g sweetened chestnut purée (about half a tin)
- 1 tbsp orange liqueur, brandy or rum
- 300 ml whipping cream
- 60 g good dark chocolate, to melt and drizzle on the log
- decorations: icing sugar, gold and silver balls, edible gold powder
- standard Swiss roll tin, lined with baking parchment

This makes a standard Swiss roll-sized cake.

A Christmas log made from chocolate is a great alternative to the more traditional Christmas cake, and I guarantee it will all be eaten long before February.

Whisk together the sugar and egg yolks until pale and fluffy. Add the cocoa and whisk again until it is fully absorbed. In a separate bowl, whisk the egg whites until stiff. Fold a tablespoonful of whites through the cocoa mix to slacken it, and fold the rest in gently.

Preheat the oven to 180°C.

Pour the mixture into the tin and bake for 20 minutes. It will rise in the oven, then fall when you take it out, but don't worry.

Leave in the tin to cool.

In a bowl, stir the alcohol into the chestnut purée. You need to taste it to ensure that you can detect its presence, but try not to make the purée too runny. Whip the cream in another bowl until stiff.

Turn out the sponge on to a clean tea cloth and remove the paper. Spread the chestnut purée over the sponge, and then spread the cream. When it's evenly spread, roll up the sponge using the cloth and put it on a plate. Don't worry if it cracks – that only makes it look more log-like.

Dredge with icing sugar, and then drizzle with the melted dark chocolate. I sprinkled with gold and silver balls and edible gold powder while the chocolate was still tacky.

Yule log

New Year's Eve: Wassail...
31 December

Here we come a-wassailing
Among the leaves so green,
Here we come a-wand'ring
So fair to be seen.
Love and joy come to you,
And to you your wassail, too,
And God bless you, and send you
A Happy New Year,
And God send you a Happy New Year.

The word 'wassail' first appears in the Anglo Saxon epic *Beowulf*, and means 'be of good health'. By the thirteenth century, the wassail bowl was used as a communal drinking vessel at a winter feast, into which revellers might dip a sweet cake or bread. The bowl might contain ale or wine, but generally it was mead or cider.

Nowadays, all around the orchards of Cornwall over Christmas and New Year there are wassailing events, harking back to the pagan past when wassailing was thought to banish any evil spirits from the orchard and ensure a good harvest. On Twelfth Night in Bodmin, four men in evening dress carry the town's applewood wassail bowl through the streets collecting for charity and singing:

Our wassail bowl is full with apples and good spice. Grant to taste it once or twice.

A report in *The Gentleman's Magazine* in 1791 gives us the words of the Wassail Song:

Here's to thee old apple tree
Whence thou mayst bud
And whence thou mayst blow!
And whence thou mayst bear apples enow
Hats full! Caps full!
And my pockets full too! Huzzah!

The words varied according to district, but the practice was fairly uniform. A group of wassailers gathered in the orchard on one of the Twelve Days of Christmas. They would bang the trees with sticks, or fire their guns into the branches. Cakes were placed as offerings, and a libation of cider poured on

to the roots of a tree. Sometimes, small bonfires were lit and the smoke would drift through the branches. A mug of hot, spiced cider was then passed around the company and the health of the trees was drunk.

Hot spiced cider

You will need:

- 1 l medium dry cider
- 2–3 tbsp honey, depending on how sweet you want it to be
- 8 whole cloves
- 4 sticks cinnamon
- half a grated nutmeg
- 8 whole allspice
- 2 star anise
- 1 unpeeled apple, thinly sliced
- 1 small orange, unpeeld, thinly sliced
- a good shot of brandy or calvados (optional)

This serves 4.

A wassail sounds like a jolly good party to me. Interestingly, it was once possible to hire wassailers if you were unable to perform the ritual yourself, and groups of young men would visit your trees in return for the usual tokens of gratitude of cider, pennies and food.

Here is a recipe for hot, spiced cider.

Warm the cider but do not boil, you don't want to waste the alcohol! Add the other ingredients, except for the brandy, and make sure the honey dissolves. Add the brandy, just before serving.

Nadelik Lowen ha Blydhen Nowydh Da! – Merry Christmas and a Happy New Year!